LIFE LESSON

KRISTINA M. MINAGLIA

LIFE LESSON

*A Testimony of God's Grace
Following an Attempted Suicide*

XULON PRESS

Xulon Press
2301 Lucien Way #415
Maitland, FL 32751
407.339.4217
www.xulonpress.com

© 2019 by Kristina M. Minaglia

All rights reserved solely by the author. The author guarantees all contents are original and do not infringe upon the legal rights of any other person or work. No part of this book may be reproduced in any form without the permission of the author. The views expressed in this book are not necessarily those of the publisher.

Unless otherwise indicated, Scripture taken from the HOLY BIBLE, NEW INTERNATIONAL VERSION. Copyright © 1973, 1978, 1984 by International Bible Society. Used by permission of Zondervan. All rights reserved.

Scripture Quotes of "Thought Starters" are taken from the NIV Thinline Bible, Busy Mom's Edition. Grand Rapids: Zondervan Publishing House, Copyright © 2009. Used by permission. All rights reserved.

To contact the author, you can send an email to authorkmm121@gmail.com or please visit: https://kminaglia121.wordpress.com/

Printed in the United States of America.

ISBN-13: 978-1-54566-652-4

DEDICATION

This book is dedicated to my son, Damon, and his late father, Thomas, who, through the will of God have changed my life forever.

I also dedicate this book to anyone facing suicidal ideation or anyone stuck in the vicious cycle of chronic homelessness, searching for hope.

Ask and it will be given to you; seek and you will find; knock and the door will be opened to you. For everyone who asks receives; the one who seeks finds; and to the one who knocks, the door will be opened. (Matt. 7:7–8 NIV)

To respect the privacy of others, names of individuals have been changed for their protection.

Thomas's real name is used with written permission.

TABLE OF CONTENTS

DEDICATION..................................v
PREFACE ix
INTRODUCTION...........................xiii

Chapter 1 –THE LORD REVEALS HIMSELF 1

Chapter 2 –SEARCHING FOR RELIEF FROM
    CHRONIC HOMELESSNESS................ 15

Chapter 3 –GOD DELIVERS FROM THE DEADLY
    GRIP OF DESOLATION 31

Chapter 4 –THE LORD REMAINS
    FAITHFUL THROUGH LIFE'S
    UNEXPECTED TURNS......................47

Chapter 5 –SINFUL DESIRES LEAD TO
    UNDESIREABLE OUTCOMES 65

Chapter 6 –STANDING FIRM IN FAITH
    OVERCOMES HARDSHIPS 77

Chapter 7 –RELY ON THE LORD TO PERSEVERE
    AGAINST EVIL 91

Chapter 8 – OBEDIENCE TO GOD AND PLACING HIM FIRST IS KEY 99

Chapter 9 – TRUST IN THE LORD WHEN THINGS DON'T GO AS EXPECTED 115

Chapter 10 – EARTH HAS NO SORROW THAT HEAVEN CANNOT HEAL (THOMAS MOORE) [2] 129

Chapter 11 – SPIRITUAL WARFARE REQUIRES DILIGENT PREPARATION 185

Chapter 12 – THERE'S NOTHING TO FEAR IN TRUSTING A SOVEREIGN GOD 203

Chapter 13 – THROWN INTO THE FIRE TO BE REFINED 217

Chapter 14 – THE LORD NEVER CEASES TO SPEAK 225

Chapter 15 – LIFE LESSONS 235

RECOMMENDED READINGS 243

NOTES 245

PREFACE

I've been told by various people I should turn my testimony into a book. This followed their review of a short story about the time I endured homelessness, which led to an attempted suicide after hitting rock bottom.

I began writing around the time my son Damon was a toddler. It was intended to be a written testimony, around twenty pages long. I wanted something for Damon to have when he got older, so he could understand his miraculous background. Quite honestly, it's an unbelievable story!

After I began to share my testimony with others, through conversations or email, lives were touched. An array of responses ranged from indifference to awe. As time went on, I recognized the need to continue to write about whatever was going on in my life—good and bad. I've been transformed by life lessons through the work of the Holy Spirit.

Throughout the course of my writing journey, I learned what my purpose is. This experience must be written for God's glory, so He could receive others into His eternal kingdom. I know for a fact this story will save lives. The Lord confirmed it one night as I lay my head down on the pillow, ready to pass out from exhaustion.

He spoke the words: *"The longer you wait, the more lives are at stake. Write that down because you'll forget what you heard."* Being a faithful servant, I complied. His words gave me the push I needed to focus on completing our task.

While I'm not sure I have the capabilities to write a book, I do feel it's important to have written documentation of my experiences to never forget where I came from. It's also good for others to see the goodness of a merciful and kind God who had compassion on me during even the darkest of times. I'll share my story with anyone and have already shared it with many. God saved my life personally twice—at the cross of Christ and on that black metal park bench.

It's by miracle alone I'm still here today to tell others no matter what happens in life, suffering isn't permanent. There'll always be hope, even when you hit rock bottom and all seems hopeless.

Through the many "life lessons" I endure in life, I recognize they all help draw me closer to my heavenly Father. He teaches me not only how to make it through, but to see the purpose in the aftermath. This story is my personal journey in how I grew closer in relationship with the Lord. I consider this to be our story, and no matter what happens, it'll ultimately have a happy ending.

To God be the glory!

INTRODUCTION

Thoughts of suicide had come and gone since my teenage years, but I never thought there'd come a point where I'd act on it. The point in my life when I felt abandoned, even by God Himself. I felt hated and despised by the world. It seemed my life was worthless, meaningless, hopeless, and without purpose, and the world would be a better place without me in it. The fateful night I took sixteen sleeping pills was not something I'd ever anticipated to actually follow through in my twenty two years on Earth.

I knew what it was like to be without the necessities in life—food, shelter and water. I was hungry. I was thirsty. I was tired. I had nowhere to go and nowhere to turn. My resources had been exhausted. What else could I do? I figured the only way out would be to take my life because things were just not getting better, no matter how hard I tried.

Little did I know, God had other plans. He had something greater in store I never, in my wildest dreams, saw coming.

There are four Scripture verses which define the turning point in my life to where I can say with strong confidence that God is real, He loves me, He is for me, and He consistently works through *all* circumstances:

> For he will deliver the needy who cry out, the afflicted who have no one to help. He will take pity on the weak and the needy and save the needy from death. He will rescue them from oppression and violence, for precious is their blood in his sight. (Psa. 72:12–14 NIV)

> I waited patiently for the Lord; he turned to me and heard my cry. He lifted me out of the slimy pit, out of the mud and mire; he set my feet on a rock and gave me a firm place to stand. He put a new song in my mouth, a hymn of praise to our God. Many will see and fear the Lord and put their trust in him. (Psa. 40:1–3 NIV)

> Praise be to the Lord, for he has heard my cry for mercy. The Lord is my strength and my shield; my heart trusts in him, and he helps me. My heart leaps for joy, and with my song I praise him. (Psa. 28:6–7 NIV)

> "For a brief moment I abandoned you, but with deep compassion I will bring you back. In a surge

of anger, I hid my face from you for a moment, but with everlasting kindness I will have compassion on you," says the Lord your Redeemer. (Isa. 54:7–8 NIV)

I also know the powers of darkness and spiritual forces of evil are real. You may not believe it, but I saw Satan himself with my own eyes at exactly 3:00 a.m. in June 2005. He was getting ready to take me to the fiery pits of hell the night I slept outside on a cold, hard, black metal park bench, attempting to put an end to my misery. He caught me in my weakest moment and chose to attack full force. Little did he know El Shaddai ("God Almighty") had something else in mind. At the time, I wasn't familiar with the Bible verses that instruct believers in how to deal with spiritual warfare:

Put on the full armor of God, so that you can take your stand against the devil's schemes. For our struggle is not against flesh and blood, but against the rulers, against the authorities, against the powers of this dark world and against the spiritual forces of evil in the heavenly realms. Therefore, put on the full armor of God, so that when the day of evil comes, you may be able to stand your ground, and after you have done everything, to stand. (Eph. 6:11–13 NIV)

> Submit yourselves, then, to God. Resist the devil, and he will flee from you. Come near to God and he will come near to you. (Jas. 4:7–8 NIV)

For someone who's stubborn and prideful like me, it took a traumatic, life altering experience to turn my life around and set me onto the straight and narrow path leading to life everlasting. It required divine intervention and an ocean of grace, compassion, mercy, and love to open my eyes, mind, and heart to my Creator.

I once heard a simple, yet profound explanation about conversion from a pastor. He said what people need is a personal encounter with Jesus to reach down and touch their hearts. The only way a person will experience conversion is through a personal encounter with Jesus.

Everything that transpired in my life has been a part of God's plan long before I even came to existence. I wasn't always a follower of Christ. The meaning of my name, Kristina, in Greek and in Swedish is "Christian." This was the name chosen for me at birth. It seems I was meant to become a Christian!

One thing I can confirm is the Lord wanted me to write about my experiences to share my testimony to others who may be experiencing traumatic, life altering experiences. It took years to learn what my purpose entailed.

Both my parents had thoughts of suicide in their younger years. By God's divine intervention, mercy, and grace, those thoughts didn't turn into action. And to those who hate their lives and are contemplating a way to end it all, please don't. I know what that pain is like.

There's much more to life than what we see in front of us. Once your perspective is changed, you'll start to see the world differently, in the way God does. You may be wondering—how does your perspective change? The answer is simple—ask Him to help.

> And we know that in all things God works for the good of those who love him, who have been called according to his purpose. For those God foreknew he also predestined to be conformed to the image of his Son, that he might be the firstborn among many brothers and sisters. And those he predestined, he also called; those he called, he also justified; those he justified, he also glorified. (Rom. 8:28–30 NIV)

1

THE LORD REVEALS HIMSELF

When someone goes through something, and they can't comprehend how or why it happened, how do you explain it? The events in which I start my story made no sense at all, but I realize we're not meant to understand everything. This is something more. It's the true story of my suffering a hell on Earth, which turned into my testimony as a believer in the one true God I have learned to love with all my heart and fear simultaneously.

I choose to begin my story by detailing a tough, traumatic experience that changed my perspective and taught me a great deal about the world. I want to make it clear I don't regret these experiences you are about to read. These experiences led me to become the person I am today. All of what you're about to read is from my own perspective. There are two sides to every story.

While putting this story together, I felt convicted to revise it, in order to not put a bad light on one of the main characters—Thomas. It took years for me to recognize had I not met him, my testimony would be nonexistent. In addition, it took about twelve years for me to truly forgive him and let go of what transpired.

Had I not endured such hardships, my perspective would remain off course. If none of this took place, God only knows where I'd be today. I can guarantee you my life wouldn't be as wonderful as I see it now. I don't have the perfect life, but I have a perfect God who is with me each step of the way, no matter what trials may come.

Sometimes I wonder how it is we only learn through tough times. The truth is, they make us stronger and wiser. Why couldn't they be simpler, or easier? I truly believe if life were fair and simple, we wouldn't need God to turn to or rely on. We need His love, support, discipline, guidance, and strength, and these can only be found in Him and His Word. "Blessed is the one who perseveres under trial because, having stood the test, that person will receive the crown of life that the Lord has promised to those who love him" (Jas. 1:12 NIV).

Before my trials, I didn't know this. I knew *of* God, but I didn't *know* Him. As a child, I believed He existed through my Catholic education and upbringing, but as I got older and entered into a public junior high school, I felt I needed proof. I couldn't see God, so how could He exist? I wanted something visual to get me to believe. There was always a sense of fear deep down I could be wrong. "The fear of the Lord is the beginning of wisdom" (Psa. 111:10 NIV).

My behaviors were quite different before the transformation process. For example, patience was almost nonexistent in my own little world. If someone spoke to me or treated me disrespectfully, I'd give them a piece of my mind, not caring if I hurt their feelings. Road rage was a regular struggle, and vulgar language was a common occurrence. I can't even count the number of times I said the Lord's name in vain.

Agnosticism was my worldview until I was approximately twenty years old. It's funny how it took a pink rosary I picked up from a sidewalk to get me to think *Maybe this is a sign.* I don't know why this thought came to mind at the time. I'll back up a little bit to start off how this all began.

I was naïve in my young adult years, coming from a sheltered childhood. I didn't know or understand the world in its true state. My parents were overprotective. Dating was something I started to do at nineteen years old, and the people I dated were not of good character. In fact, the first one went ahead and pushed intercourse on me despite my wishes against it.

I was proud to be a virgin, and to have my virginity taken by someone without my consent affected me for many years. Things didn't work out with this individual, so I cut him out of my life. Similar circumstances became repetitious in those years. I allowed evil into my life without understanding the emotional consequences that'd follow. Like I said, I was naïve.

Later on, I developed feelings for someone on the internet I had been talking to for a few years. His name was Thomas. I believe we started talking off and on when I was about eighteen years old. His internet screen name was "angelic demon 666." I thought it was a little bizarre, but he seemed to be a nice guy, and I enjoyed talking to him because he was interesting. We'd talk on the phone for hours.

Thomas said he was in a gang and wanted to get out. He claimed he almost got killed, and it was extremely dangerous for him on the east coast where he resided. This worried me, so I told him, "Why don't you move to Kenosha and stay with me?" I recently moved into my own studio apartment at twenty years old.

He said, "You can't leave me if I move there because I'm leaving everything I know to go across the country to live with you." I told him I wouldn't leave him. He agreed to the idea and took the bus to Kenosha.

We met for the first time in April 2003, and it was nerve wracking. I feared the unexpected and started to second guess my offer, but it was too late. I was already in love with him, and he was here now. After a while, I thought he would've found work to be able to help contribute to his share of expenses. He said it was hard to find work in Kenosha, and I believed him. Little did I know how long this would be going on, and I'm not sure he really looked for work.

Before I continue, it's best to say the remainder of these few chapters are what I remembered at the time. Some things have gone from my memory, and I believe the reason is I'm not meant to remember details of a few things I was told during this experience. I think it's safe to say I was oblivious to mental health issues, resulting from my naivety. You'll see what I mean.

So back to the rosary on the ground I mentioned earlier. I found it one day while we were out for a walk. Not too long after that, I woke up one morning and heard Thomas talk to someone in his sleep. I don't remember what he said, but when he woke up shortly after, he told me the archangel Michael came to him in his sleep and wanted to talk to me.

I thought about the "sign" I came across before. I was in shock. Why would the archangel Michael want to talk to *me*? Now this is the part I mentioned earlier about how to explain something you don't understand.

Michael started talking to me, through Thomas. From what I remember, I was told many things, one of which included, "The Big Guy upstairs wanted to talk to me." What in the world was going on? I was asked if I wanted to be a saint but was warned that with this comes suffering. I'd have to suffer for a little while in order for this to happen. Without understanding what being a saint entailed, I agreed to it.

For your reference, Easton's biblical definition of *saint* is "one separated from the world and consecrated to God; one holy by profession and by covenant; a believer in Christ." [1]

I was then told to bow to the floor, close my eyes and not look up, or I'd die from looking because God was in my presence. At the time, I didn't know much about the Bible. There's a story in 1 Samuel 6, which described how the people of Beth Shemesh handled the presence of the Lord through the ark of the covenant. They didn't handle God's presence appropriately and gazed upon the ark, which caused them to die.

> But God struck down some of the inhabitants of Beth Shemesh, putting seventy of them to death because they looked into the ark of the Lord. The people mourned because of the heavy blow the Lord had dealt them. And the people of Beth Shemesh asked, "Who can stand in the presence of the Lord, this holy God? To whom will the ark go up from here?" (1 Sam. 6:19–20 NIV)

The Lord's presence is powerful and precarious. I'm glad I didn't give in to the temptation of looking up as He spoke. He talked to me and told me things. I don't remember what exactly, but this new experience was unbelievable. Out of the billions of people in the world, why me? What made me so special?

Things weren't too bad at first. He asked me to do inconvenient tasks. I didn't mind doing them because I was doing them for God! Then, things began to get a little bit worse. This is where I think Satan stepped in.

One day, I saw Thomas smoking something from a pipe. I was clueless when it came to drugs. He told me it was "ambrosia," and he needed to smoke it. Eventually, I learned it was crack cocaine. During this time, the devil started to communicate to me through Thomas. Satan is the father of all lies and deception, and I didn't realize what his underlying plan was during this time.

While in my relationship to Thomas, I came across a lot of new people, most of whom were drug dealers and addicts whom I'd never associate with prior to this. I didn't like them, either, so I figured this was part of my suffering and to deal with it. What really upset me was when Thomas and his new friend Bill took my car to go on drug runs. I stayed home because it was late at night when they went, and I thought, *What if the cops catch them*? Pretty soon, I lived in paranoia.

Then he wanted my money, more and more of it. If I bought something, I'd have to return it for the money back and give it to Thomas so he could buy his "ambrosia." I was told if I didn't do what he said, bad things would happen, and he was detailed about them, too. I figured God was putting me through a test, and I had to do what I was told. I developed a different kind of fear of God.

One of the most bizarre things I witnessed occurred after giving Thomas all of my money, which left me broke. We needed something to eat, and there wasn't much food in the house. Money didn't go to anything except crack cocaine. If I "passed a test" as he would call it, he coughed up money. As crazy as it sounds, I saw coins, and once in a while, dollar bills come out of his mouth. I was in shock at what I witnessed, but I thanked God for the blessing and bought something to eat. I still can't comprehend how he was able to do it. It's something you have to see for yourself to believe.

Another thing he had me do was write bad checks at a gas station. I had to go daily or sometimes twice a day to write checks for $20.00 over what I owed for cash to support his drug use. His addiction increased my debt in various ways. I took out a payday loan, not being able to pay it back. I cosigned a cell phone for him, and the bills were never paid. This resulted in getting billed $800.00 as cosigner. The debt continued to increase.

Just when I thought my suffering reached its peak, it got worse. In September 2003, I was on my way to work in Racine. While in my car, I looked in the rearview mirror and saw a pickup truck swerving in and out of lanes, driving carelessly. He came up swift and close before he cut over the next lane to pass me up. I thought he was going to hit me!

At the time, I had road rage issues. I drove up next to him and flipped him off. This made him angry as he obviously had road rage, too. He then cut me off and tried to run me off the road. If I hadn't braked, he would've hit me for sure; that's how close he was. As I tried to catch my wheel and get straight on the road, he did it again! This time, I lost control and started fishtailing. Somehow, he ended up right next to me, and I couldn't control my car anymore. It hit the side of his truck, and I spun off to the ditch on the side of the road.

Thankfully, he pulled over. It was midmorning, and a lot of people were out on their way to work. The police showed up a little later. Witnesses called in to report the accident, confirming it was his fault. I know I shouldn't have flipped him off. I was upset, but there was hope. His auto insurance was going to pay for my damages.

I called my parents to let them know what happened. They allowed me to borrow their car until I got mine fixed in order to have transportation for work. Thomas and Bill started driving my parent's car, doing the same thing they had done with mine.

At this point Bill also started hitting on me, which made me uncomfortable. I brought it up with Thomas, and we decided we were going to stop talking to him. There was something not right with this guy, and I had a bad feeling about him.

One night in October of 2003, we heard someone pounding on the door downstairs while we were trying to sleep. It was Bill, and he kept calling out Thomas's name. My apartment was upstairs, and I kept the entry door on the first floor locked. The lights were off, and we pretended to be asleep. I peeked out the window and saw him walking away with another guy, looking upset. I thought, *What a psychopath*.

Not even five minutes later, I heard a loud smash. I looked out the window and saw Bill and his accomplice running away, carrying what looked like a bat. I looked at my parent's car and saw the passenger side windows were smashed, and the tires were flat. I called the police right away and told them what I knew about Bill. That was when I found out he wasn't allowed in Kenosha and was on probation.

Thankfully, I had money to buy used tires, and a coworker put them on for me. Soon after, I had the windows fixed, too. My dad became impatient with me using his car and wondered what took so long. I gave his car back once it looked back to normal. I feared how he'd react if he found out what happened. I never felt as desperate as I did at this time. Little did I know worse was still to come.

Thomas convinced me the mechanics would take longer to fix my car if I gave them the money first. I decided to hold off in paying them. He then told me to cash the $4,000 check and give it to him. I gave it to him out of fear in having to do what he told me. I never saw the money or my car again. Looking back now, I feel ashamed of how gullible I was.

This series of events happened all within a few short months. Following the accident and my parents' car getting damaged, my dad found out who I was dating and disowned me. I didn't tell anyone about Thomas's drug problem because I kept certain things a secret. I didn't understand what made my dad upset. He told me I was never to see my family again.

Twelve years later, my dad finally told me what made him angry. He looked up Thomas's name, which was a common name, and came across information leading him to become enraged. If I would've known that from the beginning, I'm sure our conflict wouldn't have escalated to the point it did. In those twelve years, I never understood why he reacted the way he did.

I immediately lost my job as a result of not having transportation from Kenosha to Racine and was forced to quit. The city bus wasn't an option, and those I thought I could count on turned their backs on me. This was the time where I realized who my true friends were. I was becoming desperate, and all I heard were excuses to why they couldn't help me.

This was extremely distressing. The next thing I was going to lose was my apartment. What was I going to do with all my belongings? Around this time, we came across an old acquaintance of mine, Mark. He lived pretty close to us and needed help, too. We decided we'd share his two bedroom apartment and everything would be fine once we established employment. Only none of us found a job. I remained calm throughout this struggle because I knew God would take care of me.

After a little while, Mark started changing. He drank more, and Thomas followed. They bought cheap beer and smoked cigarettes in the apartment all day long, which put me over the edge. Mark started to treat me differently, his attitude grew worse toward me, and Thomas didn't do anything about it. I felt miserable and physically sick to my stomach.

One day, Thomas and I were arguing about the current situation, and Mark walked up to my face, instigating trouble. It appeared he wanted me to hit him and stood there smirking at me. I didn't like my personal space invaded and never allowed anyone to disrespect me, so I hit him. Just to be clear, I didn't go around hitting people. This was an isolated incident.

After I hit him, he walked to a payphone to call the police. I didn't care, it felt good to stand up for myself. When the police arrived, one officer spoke to me, and the other spoke to Mark separately. Thomas had left the scene. I admitted I hit Mark in the face. I proceeded to tell the police about how poorly he treated me and how he instigated trouble all the time. While Mark thought I was going to jail, he ended up wasting the officers' time.

One day, Mark's relatives came over, and it seemed like they tried to do an intervention. Everything said that night is unclear to me now, but what I do remember is they called my parents and told them we all looked high. I've *never* done drugs before. At this point, I was beyond stressed out living there and decided I'd be better off sleeping in the streets. I packed up what I needed in two duffel bags and left with Thomas. I was relieved to be able to escape this dysfunctional living arrangement.

2

SEARCHING FOR RELIEF FROM CHRONIC HOMELESSNESS

The temperature was cold, and it snowed the night we left Mark's apartment. Thomas and I looked for somewhere warm to sleep and managed to find a sheltered bus stop near the police station to rest in. I shivered as I put my arms inside my coat sleeves and dug my face inside my coat collar. I tried to make the best of it. A police officer drove by and saw us sitting there. I wonder why he didn't stop to tell us about any shelters. Maybe he didn't realize we didn't have anywhere to go. I'll give him the benefit of the doubt. The beginning of my homeless experience took place January of 2004, right before my twenty first birthday.

During the day, Thomas and I went to the library to keep warm from the weather outside. Eventually, we came across a day shelter, which fed the homeless. They told us about a local homeless shelter program. Each night, the homeless slept at a different church throughout the city. I was relieved to find out there was somewhere else to sleep besides the outdoors.

One of the unfortunate aspects of the shelters was only one or two churches had a shower to use. If we were lucky enough to get there early and have a spot, I'd go in the bathroom to wash up. I washed my hair in the sink, and as crazy as it sounds, I kept the blow dryer in my bag to blow dry my hair. I was homeless, but I did not want to look it! I even kept my makeup and put it on daily like usual.

The shelters operated the same for each of the churches. Everyone had a mat to sleep on, and we put linens on once we arrived. Women slept on one side of the room and men on the other. Thankfully there were volunteers keeping an eye out because it's really scary not knowing who's there and what they're capable of doing.

Once in a while there'd be a TV on or a movie playing. I remember playing bingo and eating snacks. They always served dinner and made a lunch for the next day. I wasn't fond of the lunches because they were either peanut butter and jelly or bologna and butter.

It was during this time I understood the truth of the phrase "beggars can't be choosers." You learn to appreciate the little things when you have nothing. In all honesty, I didn't care for either of those sandwiches for the longest time because they brought back flashbacks of this experience.

I went to the local day shelter daily. One of the owners told people they could leave their duffel bags there instead of carrying them around with them. Since I carried two bags, I decided to leave one.

I didn't notice at first anything was missing from my bags, but one day a volunteer came in wearing one of my favorite shirts. I knew it was mine, too. I asked her where she got it, and she said it was on a table in back with a bunch of other things. I was exasperated. Those I know from the shelter told me later on that the two in charge of the day shelter were taking donations for themselves, not to mention the belongings of those who were homeless.

Transportation was hard to come by. Occasionally I was able to obtain bus tokens. Other times we were able to get a ride from someone who had a car. But if you didn't have either of those options, you walked. I did a *lot* of walking. It was your only choice if you wanted to get to those shelters early. The shelters only had so much room, and if you didn't make it before they ran out of mats, you were turned away.

During the day, my home was the library. I kept busy by searching the newspaper and internet for jobs. I also read magazines to keep my mind off the suffering. People wondered how I could have a smile on my face when homeless. I knew God was taking care of me, and this test wasn't permanent.

At some point, I came across a book, which revealed the importance of being a dreamer during traumatic events. I tend to be an idealist and think of what could be. If I looked at the reality of what was going on, who knows how I could've been negatively impacted. There were times I felt like I could end up in the mental hospital.

For example, not long after I met Thomas and experienced an increase in suffering, I banged my head on the wall and stabbed a loaf of bread with a knife because I just couldn't take what was going on. I know it sounds crazy, but if you were in my shoes, you'd understand.

I believed a lot of what Thomas told me, even though they were bizarre statements. He told me unusual things about the Bible and the book of Revelation. I'd rather not go into those details. At this point, I don't recall much of it, anyway. I believed him because he had me convinced it was coming from something "divine."

He led me to fear there were people watching us, and some were out to hurt me. For instance, before I was evicted from my apartment and we called the police on Bill, I truly believed he had people hang around my apartment and feared for my safety. Thankfully nothing ever happened. In the most vulnerable and dangerous situations, I always remained safe. Praise be to the Lord.

One day, I heard about a job opportunity. The position was for a teacher at a daycare down the road from the day shelter. I ended up getting hired and was grateful to finally find a job. There was hope for stability and security. Unfortunately, I still didn't get to keep most of the money I made.

There were times when we didn't go to the shelter and had to sleep outside. It was embarrassing because of the risk of being seen by an onlooker or the police. I know someone saw us one cold night when we slept next to the church I worked at. It was always cold when I had to sleep outside. I think one of those nights, it even rained a little. This time period is a little blurry to me.

Another outdoor experience occurred on a snowy winter night. Once again, we had to find somewhere to sleep with absolutely nowhere to go. Thomas had become friends with a man named Ben who also had a crack addiction and lived with his girlfriend. He decided we would sneak into their basement and sleep there. I believe it was accessible from the outside, which was how we got in. It was the kind of basement you'd picture in a nightmare. It was scary, dirty, and freezing cold. Thankfully, we had somewhere inside to sleep. I was afraid we'd get caught, but we didn't.

I'll never forget this particular night because of how disgusted and ashamed I felt. It had been hours since I had access to a bathroom. I had no other choice but to urinate on the basement floor in the corner. How repulsive.

Even though I had to occasionally sleep outdoors, I still made sure to clean up in a bathroom somewhere. I carried toiletries with me in a duffel bag, which were given out at the shelters. I was grateful for the homeless shelters because they provided somewhere to sleep, something to eat, and people to talk to. If not for them, I would've either frozen or starved to death.

I took many things for granted throughout my life, but God revealed what true gratitude is. I learned to appreciate things in a different way. During this time, I had much to learn. God began to mold me by breaking down my pride and weaving in humility.

One day, I came across some good news. My coworker was selling her house. They moved most of their belongings out, with the exception of a couch still left in the basement. She said we could stay there temporarily, and I expressed appreciation. It was a distance from work, but I didn't mind walking to and from work each day. Eventually, I obtained a bike somehow and was able to ride it to work.

During our stay at the house, I frequented the local bars. There were times when I drank so much, I didn't remember what happened that night. The truth of the matter is it was an unhealthy coping mechanism to deal with the chaos in my life. I hated the hangovers and vomiting, yet I continued to do it.

One night, I went out with Ben's girlfriend and drank two Long Island Iced Teas and blacked out. She drove me to their home, and I remember briefly opening my eyes to Ben carrying me upstairs with Thomas right behind him, where they put me on the couch. When I woke up, they told me I threw up all over my arm, and they cleaned me up. I would've never known, given my level of intoxication. I'm glad this couple was trustworthy. If not, who knows what could've happened?

Our stay at my coworker's house eventually came to an end. We then moved into a three bedroom apartment, which was unnecessary for us, but I knew the landlord from work. I was relieved to have my own place again, but deep down, I had a feeling it wasn't going to last.

I have one memory living here. Thomas asked me to go to the neighbor for money. I was employed, but my money rarely made it to things that were priority, like rent and food. I absolutely did not want to ask the neighbor for money, but Thomas threatened me.

It hurt my pride to ask a stranger for money. If I remember correctly, I cried as I asked. Not to get pity, but because I really did not want to do this and was horribly ashamed. He gave it to me, though—twenty dollars, which would go to an "eight ball" of crack.

As previously mentioned, I knew our stay here wasn't going to last. The rent wasn't paid, and it was about time to get evicted. I don't remember much about what occurred between our stay here and the next place, but it was time to move on and find somewhere else to live.

I recall another coworker telling me about a low cost rooming house downtown near the daycare, so I went and put an application in. The only problem was the room was for one occupant. I had to sneak Thomas in. I didn't care too much for the manager because he made me uncomfortable. He was always drunk and often hit on me. He lived onsite.

One night, a friend of Thomas's came to the rooming house to see if he was home. Carl was an addict who often talked to himself and heard voices. I told Carl Thomas wasn't home, and he decided to wait for him there. It was in this moment where I was asked to do crack for the first time.

I told Carl I didn't smoke, and he knew this. He replied, "No one has to know; you don't have to tell Thomas." I still refused. I thank God I never had the curiosity to experiment with drugs. It saddens me to see people fall prey to that kind of evil.

Working at the daycare became increasingly stressful for me. It seemed like they were trying to find reasons to get rid of me. They couldn't fire me because they knew I was a good teacher and was well liked by the children and parents. I followed the rules and did what I was supposed to. It came to the point where I was fed up and couldn't take it anymore.

One morning, I had the kids lined up for a bathroom break, and I don't remember the reason, but the supervisor got on my case. A coworker didn't like something I said, and at the time I didn't care what I said or who I said it to. I was tired of being the topic of gossip and discriminated against by some of my coworkers. After arguing with the supervisor, I said, "Fine, I don't have to put up with this anymore!" and I walked out the door.

I cried, knowing I was in a situation where I desperately needed a job, but the stress was affecting me mentally and emotionally. I used my last paycheck to buy a $400 van. Not long after, I was evicted from the rooming house. I couldn't pay rent because I never got to keep my own money, and the manager found out Thomas was living with me.

One night, the manager brought the landlord over. He was shouting at me about the eviction. I was surprised at how unprofessionally he was handling this. I packed what I could in the van and left.

Thomas convinced me to move to Racine because he claimed the shelters were better out there. The shelter program in Racine was, in fact, better, but there were more homeless people in Racine then there were in Kenosha. I was happy to hear we were able to go to the family fitness club for free. Since they had showers there, I was able to shower daily.

I began searching for a new job, this time in Racine, but to no avail. I went to the library daily because it was the only place I had to go. It was quite difficult applying for jobs with no physical address or contact number.

While unemployed, I was able to earn a little bit of income by donating plasma. I received somewhere around $25.00 twice a week. If I was lucky, I got to keep $5.00 of it. Thomas always wanted $20.00 for an eight ball of crack.

To make matters worse, my van started to break down on me. It was in pretty good condition when I purchased it, but shortly after Thomas told me he thought he hit a curb, I found out there was a transmission fluid leak. It was a struggle trying to continuously fill it with transmission fluid and fuel, just to keep it running.

Around April 2005, we had no other choice but to sleep in the van. The shelters were only open during the winter months. I was glad I saved blankets from the shelters because it was really cold at night.

I heard about a place, which served breakfast Sunday mornings and decided to go there. The lady in charge talked with us, and we told her our situation. I cried after letting it out, and she kindly offered for us stay there. She allowed me to stay in a bedroom upstairs with her teenage granddaughters. There were also other men living in the building, who needed shelter and worked for her.

Within the same week, she began to treat me differently. It felt like I was in a prison. There were strict rules where you couldn't leave without permission, and I heard I was lucky to be able to leave a few times. How could anyone get back on their feet if they were being forced to stay with her all the time? I decided to leave because I was tired of being treated like a prisoner. The van was home yet again for a little while.

I continued to think things couldn't get any worse, but they did. Thomas became friends with another crack addicted drug dealer, Scott. We ended up sleeping at Scott's house, which was infested with all kinds of bugs, including cockroaches. I tried to imagine they weren't there, so I could sleep. It was a nightmare. Little did I know what was going on behind my back.

One night while I was in bed pretending to sleep, I overheard Thomas and Scott talk about selling my van. That was all I had left! I got out of bed to find out two drug dealers who I hadn't met before, claimed Thomas owed them money and wouldn't return my van until he paid them back. They left in my van that had all my belongings in it.

I called the police and told them what happened. The van was still leaking transmission fluid, so they couldn't get far without it breaking down. The police later updated me saying they found my van parked, and someone was sleeping inside. It was Thomas. How was I supposed to respond to this? He knew where my van was all along while I panicked, thinking it was stolen. Once I got it back, I took off and never returned.

For the next several weeks, we slept in the van. I was unable to get it out of the downtown area because it always died on me. Thomas's addiction continued to take precedence over our basic needs. The hardest part of living in the van was trying to park away from the meters and out of police radar.

One night, we got stuck near the lake, and I remember waking up to a flashlight in the window. Two police officers told us we had to move the van, but it wouldn't even start. How much more embarrassment could I take from this? Eventually, the van started, and we moved it to where the police suggested. I thanked God for getting us there.

During this time, we would go to what they called "meal sites." They took place in various churches every evening for dinner. The list we had wasn't up to date because two of the seven churches listed weren't open. This meant two days out of the week, I wasn't able to eat.

On one unforgettable night in April 2005, Thomas and I sat in my parked van, facing the lake. I'm not sure exactly who asked me this question because throughout the entire time in knowing Thomas, there were different "beings" talking to me from heaven and from hell, telling me things through him. It won't make sense unless you were there, experiencing it.

Anyway, I was asked the question, "If you had a child and had the choice to end your suffering by putting the remainder of your suffering on your child or finish it yourself, which would you choose?" I said, "Of course I'd finish it myself;

why would I ever want my child to suffer?" I didn't think much of this question until a few months down the road. I'll explain later.

As usual, the van broke down. I had around $10.00 to fill up the gas can and get a couple bottles of transmission fluid, so I could move the van. Unfortunately, Thomas had something else in mind. He wanted the money. He fought me with a crazy look in his eyes, intent on getting the money from me. I ran away from him and screamed. I tried to lock myself in the van, but I wasn't fast enough. I'm only 5'2" and he was 6'2". I continued screaming as he got the money and walked off.

I couldn't take living like this anymore. At this point, things were never getting better, only worse and worse. Worrying about my van breaking down, sleeping in it, and giving into Thomas's addiction were all getting to my head. I was severely depressed, and suicidal thoughts raced through my mind. Things seemed hopeless, but whenever I felt this way, something would come up to give me a tiny piece of hope.

There was a shelter in Racine for women with children in the process of being taken over by another organization. The women's shelter was going to close once the new one was up and running. A woman heading the program asked if I wanted to help clean a few rooms for a little bit of money. I took advantage of the opportunity and found out they let some people stay in motel rooms while the new shelter was under construction. The program we previously participated in was now closed permanently. This new organization was going to open up one whole shelter for men, women, and children.

The director of the new organization let us stay in one of the motel rooms for a few weeks. Thomas and I somehow devised a plan we were going to move to Florida. It appeared there were better opportunities, and it looked like a nice place to live. Thomas told me he was saving money, so we could take a bus there one way. He claimed he was doing an under the table job, which was on a first come, first served basis, but I never saw the money.

During our stay at the motel, I scrapped my van for $50.00. I was under the impression we were going to leave town shortly. We were supposed to purchase bus tickets with the money, but Thomas immediately got hold of most of it. I used the remaining funds for food, but it wasn't much. The meal sites were too far away from the motel, and I was getting too weak to walk to them, being famished.

There was nothing for me to eat, and it got to the point where a quarter became of significant value to me because it meant I could go to the gas station to buy a small, sugary snack. This was sometimes breakfast, lunch, or dinner. I drank a lot of water from the bathroom faucet in the motel room. I inevitably became sick as a result of malnutrition.

Our two week stay at the motel came to an end, and every last bit of hope drifted off into the abyss. I had nothing in my possession except a bag of clothes. The outdoors were going to be my new home—this time, permanently. It was the end of June 2005, and I had nowhere to sleep, nothing to eat, no hope of getting a job, no transportation, no family or friends, and no reason to live.

3

GOD DELIVERS FROM THE DEADLY GRIP OF DESOLATION

It was time to end this misery once and for all. I devised a plan to commit suicide and was set on following through with it. The plan required a little bit of money, so I decided to donate plasma one last time. Half of the money went to Thomas, even after I told him my plan. You don't quite realize the devastating effect drugs have on a person until you experience the way in which the addict prioritizes. Crack cocaine was more important than my life.

I went to a sandwich shop downtown and ordered my "last meal." Then, I walked over to the pharmacy, searching for sleeping pills. I debated which brand of sleeping pills to buy. Little did I know this choice would *greatly* affect the future.

I think I chose the generic brand because it was cheaper. I don't know why it mattered because they were all going to do the same thing, I had hoped, in the end.

I carried the pills in my purse and walked over to a bench, facing Lake Michigan. I told Thomas earlier where I was going to sleep that night before he took off, so he knew where I was going to be. I don't know why it mattered, but I told him anyway.

It was still daylight. I began to take the pills slowly, using saliva to swallow them, since I had no water bottle. It was an awful feeling. I hated taking pills, but taking them with a dry mouth made it feel much worse.

As the sun set and it grew dark, I walked over to the spot I chose to sleep. I came across a metal bench near the library, somewhat hidden where no one would be able to see me. Thomas found me later on, and I told him what I was doing. He yelled at me and stormed off. I believe he went to do drugs at someone's house and stayed the night there. I never felt more alone.

Altogether, I took about sixteen of the twenty four sleeping pills and became extremely tired. As I took them, I talked to God. I remember telling Him I didn't want to do this, but there was nothing left. I had absolutely no reason to live. No one cared about where I was or what I was doing. If I was gone, no one would notice.

I begged Him to take me and end the pain. I even wished for a reason to live. I cried in such a pitiful manner. That moment was when I hit rock bottom. I felt worthless, my existence pointless, and there was no hope anymore. The last two years were a *living hell*, and though I was told it was going to be great after my suffering was done, my belief in that disappeared.

A little while later, this homeless man I knew from the shelter named Pete, saw me and asked where Thomas was. I hid the pill box in my purse and tried to act normal, as difficult as that was. I told him Thomas said he was coming back later, but he never did come back. Pete waited on the bench next to me for what felt like an eternity. He just kept talking and talking.

I didn't want him there, but eventually he left. I forced myself to stay awake because I didn't know him too well, and who knows what could've happened if I had passed out. I finally did fall asleep and hoped to never wake up again.

At 3:00 a.m., I woke up suddenly. I looked up at the clock on the building next to me to see what time it was. I don't know how I was able to wake up, but I thought I heard something. My back ached from sleeping on the metal bench. It was surprisingly cold, being the end of June. Like I said, it was always cold when I had to sleep outside. I looked up toward the sound.

At first, I thought there was a garbage bag floating around in the sky, but there was no wind. It was black, and then I saw red. As I continued looking at this strange sight, I noticed the object was circling above me and looked like a man. He had a red body, a bald head, and I don't know if there were black horns, but he had black legs and black wings. Whether it was the devil himself or one of his demons, I don't know, but something was getting ready to take me to hell. I truly believe it was Satan himself.

My heartbeat decreased significantly. I attempted to sit up, but it was difficult to do so. When I tried to stand up, my body felt numb, and I fell right back down. Those pills were doing their job, but not to completion just yet. I lay back down and begged the entity in the sky to take me.

There were previously a few occasions where I was asked to sell my soul to the devil. He asked me in the midst of the most troubling circumstances when I felt utterly hopeless. At the time, I agreed to his deal because I was upset with God for putting me through such misery.

For some reason, God always took me back. He didn't let the devil keep me. There's no way I deserved His great mercy. Little did I know at the time, but this was a battle for my soul between my loving Creator and my greatest enemy. Satan deceived me into thinking I was going to get something out of it, which I never did. The devil is a liar, whose purpose is to kill and destroy those whom God loves (John 10:10).

Satan also told me if I went to hell, I'd be treated like a queen. That thought came to mind as I saw him in the sky and begged him to take me to end my suffering on Earth. I still wonder why the devil would reveal himself to me in this way. Why did he personally torment me enough to lead me here to rock bottom, attempting to end my life? I know he doesn't reveal himself to everyone in this manner. "Your enemy the devil prowls around like a roaring lion looking for someone to devour" (1 Pet. 5:8 NIV).

I fell back asleep for a few hours and woke up around 5:00 a.m. This time I was somehow able to walk, though I still felt highly affected by the pills. I decided to go to the family fitness club to take a shower.

My plan was to wait at the library to let Thomas know I was okay. After the shower, I waited in the club lobby until the library opened. One of the employees at the lobby began talking to me. He told me he saw me around with a tall, skinny guy. I didn't recognize this man and thought it was odd how he recognized me. I revealed to him about my attempt to end my life. He wanted to take me to look for work when his shift ended. I told him I needed to wait for Thomas, so instead, he drove me around, looking for Thomas until the library opened up at 9:00 a.m.

After Thomas and I found each other, I told him I wanted to go to the hospital to get help. It was June 28, 2005. As we walked toward the hospital, we ended up getting into an argument over something, and he left. I proceeded to go to the hospital alone and saw a few women at a desk. I told them what I did and broke down in tears. It got to the point where I couldn't breathe because I cried so hard. They asked me to sit down, and the next thing I knew, paramedics took me to another hospital to get checked out.

When I arrived, staff took blood and urine tests. They inquired about which sleeping pills I took. After the tests, the doctor came back and asked me when my last regular period was. I told him I had it for one day in May, but figured the significant stress I endured made it irregular, so April was the last normal period I had. He then told me I was two months pregnant.

I was in shock. I didn't know what to think or what to do. My first thought was how foolish I was to put an innocent baby's life at risk. The doctor said if I chose the other brand of pills, it would've affected the baby, but since I took the right one, it did no harm. Like I said earlier, little did I know how critical that decision would become later on.

I felt a sense of relief. The previous night while talking to God, I wished for a reason to live, and He gave it to me. He graciously spared my life *and* gave me a reason to live. How could I have possibly deserved this? I'll never understand. The Lord performed a personal miracle without my knowledge for two months. He has a thing for perfect timing.

I somewhat relate to Hannah's story in the Bible. In 1 Samuel 1, Hannah is deeply troubled over her circumstance, being unable to bear a child for her husband and provoked by his other wife, Peninnah. She pours her heart out to the Lord in desperation, and in the midst of her sorrow, Eli the priest prayed the Lord would grant her what she asked. Afterward, Hannah was no longer sad.

Despair never has the final word. In the most desperate, hopeless circumstances, God faithfully shows up and begins to work immediately. There are several scriptures in the Bible to prove it. You may also know people whose testimonies prove how God worked in the midst of the impossible.

I personally experienced His divine intervention and believe without a doubt that God is faithful and able. We can't dig ourselves out of the miry pit alone. Our only hope is to turn to God to raise us up and place us on solid ground.

"He lifted me out of the slimy pit, out of the mud and mire; he set my feet on a rock and gave me a firm place to stand" (Psa. 40:2 NIV).

Sometimes I wonder what would've happened if I didn't talk to God that night, or if I chose the other brand of pills, or if Pete didn't come to keep me awake for hours. Would I be here today? God had it all worked out according to His divine plan, and I didn't know it at the time, as we never know what His plans are, but I thank Him for it.

The hospital discharged me to a crisis house as a suicide risk, although once I heard the news, I felt fine. I had a sense of hope again. The crisis center was a wonderful place. While I looked for work, staff provided bus tokens for transportation. I had a nice, comfortable bed to sleep in and a shower to use. I ate three meals a day. It felt like a home.

Once my time was up, the crisis center discharged me to the local shelter for women with children, the one I was previously offered money to clean. I was also referred to the job center to apply for medical insurance and food stamps. At first, I didn't like the shelter because of the strict rules and personalities of some of the women there. It was nothing to complain over because it was much better than where I had been!

This provided an opportunity to think about my future. I didn't know what to do with Thomas. I wasn't going to be homeless with a baby, and this would certainly continue if I stayed with him. As many times as I threatened to leave him, I never did. When I told him this time around, of course he didn't believe me. He gave me the usual spiel that he would change, get a job, and stop doing drugs. There was no convincing me this time.

My perspective drastically changed following this entire experience. I told Thomas if he can get his own place, work a steady job, and have his own transportation, then I'd give him a second chance. Unfortunately, his mind was set was on one thing and one thing only.

It had been a while since I made any friends, but I got along well with many of the women at the shelter. I went for a walk one day with a new friend, Penny. I don't remember where we were going, but I remember having a candy bar in one hand and juice in the other. We walked up to a stoplight and had the right of way to cross.

Penny hurried ahead of me and turned around to tell me to hurry up. As she turned to look at me, I saw something in the corner of my eye. Before I had a chance to turn my head to see what was coming, I was hit. An SUV turned the corner from behind me and hit me on the left side of my body. Penny said I flew about fifteen feet before I hit the street and rolled. Thankfully, my arm cushioned my head from hitting the street too hard. Unfortunately, I still ended up having a huge bump on my head anyway.

Everything became blurry, and I remember hearing the man who hit me talking nervously on his phone, "Yeah, I'm the one who hit her." I felt bad for him. Penny was upset, yelling at him. I sat up and screamed "I'm pregnant!" I was four months pregnant at the time.

I asked for my juice because I was thirsty, but someone told me to lay down because I was in shock. I responded with "No, the street is too dirty. I feel fine." Out of the blue, a man came up and prayed for me and the baby. I appreciated his kindness, praying for a stranger at the scene of an accident. When the ambulance arrived, they took me to the hospital. I was discharged after a few short hours with only a prescription to help with pain. I was distraught because all they did was check the baby's heartbeat and told me it'd be okay. How could they possibly know that?

Medical providers generally don't treat patients with as much care if they're covered by Medicaid. I've experienced treatment in both ends to know this is true. In my opinion, I would've received more in depth care if I had a different insurance company.

Penny stayed with me throughout this ordeal and as we talked at the bus stop near the hospital, I suddenly felt something. I told her "I felt a poke on the inside."

She said, "That's your baby kicking. He's mad that you shook him up!" I laughed feeling relieved. I was worried about the helpless child inside.

The ladies at the shelter were surprised to see not long after this accident, I was up and walking around. I felt sore on both sides, especially the left side where I got hit. I didn't want to let the accident keep me from moving on. I was tough from the inside out.

The prescribed medication suggested I eat before taking the dose. There were times I neglected the instruction and took the medication before falling asleep. This led to spitting up a clear liquid, which wasn't a pleasant feeling. Another side effect was dizziness, which made it difficult to walk up and down the stairs to get to my room.

Shortly after the accident, I received a call from the sheriff's department, notifying me about Thomas's arrest for theft. This helped me to place more focus on my priorities. I had no intention getting back with Thomas; he just didn't realize it yet.

After searching for employment, I located an easy, part time job at the mall. I saved up a majority of what I made over the span of a few months and was able to get into a transitional housing program through the shelter. The duplex apartment was in a neighborhood I wasn't too fond of, but I finally had my own place, which was good enough for me.

The previous tenant left behind a couch, a swivel rocking chair, and a few tables in the living room. I slept on the couch at first because I didn't have a bed. An employee at the shelter went to a thrift store to purchase a twin bed, which I appreciated. Slowly, my apartment began to feel like a home, as more people who wanted to help provided various items.

I couldn't believe how far I came in such a short time—from being homeless with no hope in sight on June 28 to working and moving into an apartment by November. Thomas wrote me letters from jail, saying he changed. He said he gained weight, was in a rehab program, and was going to find work when he got out. I didn't believe him this time. Those same lines got old after a while.

I recall going to court for him. He used me being pregnant as an excuse to get out of jail earlier. Shortly after he got out, he cut off his ankle bracelet and disappeared. I didn't mind the disappearance because I didn't want him to be a part of my life anymore. I especially didn't trust him with a baby.

It was now the winter season in the year 2005, and I was home alone on Christmas Day. As I washed dishes in the sink, I felt something unusual. It seemed like I peed my pants, but I knew that couldn't be. The only explanation was my water broke. I called a friend I made at the mall, Carla, to drive me to the hospital. After the nurse checked me out, she told me my water didn't break. I was discharged and went back home.

Three days later, on December 28, I went to work as usual, but this day was different. I felt funny. After my shift ended, I went to a mandatory group at the shelter, which was a requirement for transitional housing participants. I explained to the ladies in group how I felt and that I noticed something on my underwear. Some of them told me, "you're about to have the baby!" I couldn't believe it because the due date was originally for January 15, but they bumped it to January 7.

One of the shelter employees gave me a ride to the hospital. I didn't even make it to the door when the contractions started, and they were coming fast. This was at approximately 6:00 p.m. I couldn't believe how excruciating the pain was, and the contractions grew progressively worse.

I called my mom to let her know I was going into labor. I was afraid to make the call, in case my dad answered, but mom wanted to be there when I had the baby. There was no answer, so I left a voicemail. She arrived later just in time for delivery.

The nurses did what they could to speed up the delivery. Out of fear, I didn't take an epidural. Instead, I took whatever they put in your IV, and it made me sleepy. My doctor told me to push, and I must not have been doing it right. I wanted to fall asleep. She told me the baby's heartbeat was slowing down, and I needed to push him out. Thankfully, at 10:00 p.m., he came out and all was well.

It was a miracle my baby survived through starvation, sleeping pills, getting hit by a truck, not to mention the significant amount of stress I endured throughout the pregnancy. Damon was a perfectly healthy six pound, four ounce newborn baby. *Praise God*! When the nurse handed him to me, she commented "He's cute. Babies never come out cute, but he came out cute!" I couldn't help but smile.

I had no idea how to care for a newborn, but thankfully there were people there to help and give me advice. A visiting nurse named Debbie came over about once a month to check up on us. Besides being a new mother, I think the primary concern for Debbie's visit was because they suspected I'd develop postpartum depression related to the attempted suicide. Debbie offered helpful advice and brought over diapers and clothes.

I finally received the settlement from the accident and used most of the money to buy a vehicle. I bought a 1999 SUV, and it cost $6,400. I was excited to have my own transportation and stop relying on the bus. I thanked God for turning the accident into a blessing.

My employer at the mall closed the shop down shortly after I had Damon. This meant I had to search for new employment. I worked part time at a grocery store, stocking shelves, but continued to search for more stable, full time employment. In June 2006, I had an interview for a position I had no experience in at a factory. I was determined to get it because it'd provide stability.

The interview went well, but I was told they gave the job to someone else. I was discouraged. I thought surely God was going to bless me with a good job in order to take better care of Damon, but maybe it wasn't meant to be. About a month later, I received a call back asking if I'd still like a job, but it'd be second shift hours. I was ecstatic, my prayers were answered, and God showed His faithfulness yet again.

4

THE LORD REMAINS FAITHFUL THROUGH LIFE'S UNEXPECTED TURNS

In November 2006, my mom called and asked if I wanted to come over for Thanksgiving. I was taken aback and asked her if Dad was going to be there. She said, "Yeah, it was his idea." What an unexpected twist. I didn't know what to say. I assumed he was going to start an argument and told her I didn't want to deal with it, but she insisted he wasn't going to. On Thanksgiving Day, I came over for the first time in about three years. Damon was about to meet his grandpa at eleven months old. He didn't bring up anything from the past as I'd anticipated. He held Damon and played with him. Another burden was lifted.

LIFE LESSON

After my two years were up in the transitional housing program, I was able to manage paying rent and bills on my own. I continued to receive childcare assistance and food stamps. Over time, I learned how to become more independent. I contemplated furthering my education but was unsure where to start. One day, a coworker told me "You know what Krissy? You'd make a good counselor."

His comment struck me. I decided a school counselor would be a good fit and proceeded to the local technical college to inquire about enrollment. They directed me to their Human Services program, and I signed up for my first class to begin in February 2008. I was twenty five years old. After one semester, I realized this program wasn't related to what I wanted to do.

During a random conversation with a professional, I found out in order to be a school counselor, I needed a degree in social work. She told me about the college she attended that had a great social work program. I decided to transfer schools.

This particular school intimidated me because it had a great reputation, and I was a single mom who probably wouldn't be able to afford it. After speaking to a representative in the adult education office, I was soon on my way to becoming a student. I was also eligible for more financial aid. Things continued to get better as time went on.

Around late summer in 2010, I felt I needed a change in my work environment. Four years at this factory was enough, and I desired a higher income. After two weeks of searching, I received a call from a manufacturer in Milwaukee and scheduled an interview.

During the interview, I toured the facility. I inquired about training, as I was overwhelmed when observing all of the tasks performed in this job. They utilized wire schematics and more complicated blueprints. I wasn't sure if it was something I could do. My experience in manufacturing consisted of simple mechanical assembly. Electrical production was not in my list of qualifications.

I had little faith in myself, but it didn't matter what I thought. God wanted me to have this job, and He gave it to me. Part of the interview process required passing a basic math and reading test. The Foundations of Mathematics class I took a semester before paid off because I *never* would've passed the math test without it! The Lord continued to show His faithfulness. The timing couldn't have been more perfect. That's how you know something is meant to be.

The commute from Kenosha to Milwaukee became expensive and drained my energy. I decided to move to Oak Creek to lessen the load. I traveled to Milwaukee to work, Kenosha to go to school, and Racine to go to church.

People wondered how I could carry such a burden. "How can you work full time, go to school, manage the home, and raise your son alone?" Little did they know the extent of my true suffering. Even more, compared to the Cross of Christ, my sufferings don't compare. The prophet Isaiah gave a clear picture of what our Lord Jesus would endure on the cross to save us from our sin. Here's a portion of that Scripture:

> He was despised and rejected by mankind, a man of suffering, and familiar with pain. Like one from whom people hide their faces he was despised, and we held him in low esteem. Surely, he took up our pain and bore our suffering, yet we considered him punished by God, stricken by him, and afflicted. But he was pierced for our transgressions, he was crushed for our iniquities; the punishment that brought us peace was on him, and by his wounds we are healed. He was oppressed and afflicted, yet he did not open his mouth; he was led like a lamb to the slaughter, and as a sheep before its shearers is silent, so he did not open his mouth. (Isaiah 53: 3–5, 7 NIV)

That Scripture puts me back in check when I start to complain about "suffering."

While it was tough balancing my responsibilities, I was determined to be successful. I knew if I wanted to keep moving up, I had to work hard for it. I couldn't depend on anyone else, other than God, to bring me into a better place.

Two years later, my faith was put to the test. In August 2012, a conflict came up between my work and school schedule. I worked first shift and always signed up for night classes. In the upcoming fall semester, I signed up for two courses, one being a requirement for the social work major. I hadn't realized this class was scheduled in the morning.

With graduation around the corner, my dilemma entailed trying to figure out how to work around the schedule. One class required a 500 hour internship, totaling twenty five hours per week. How could I work a full time job, perform the internship, take my spring classes requiring homework, *and* have time for Damon and my household responsibilities? This impossible scenario required a difficult decision.

Like I said, my faith was put to the test. The only available option was to sacrifice my source of income. It was stressful thinking about it and as usual, the stress made me physically and emotionally sick. Deep down, I knew it was all going to work out because God never fails, no matter how hopeless things appear. His plans are always greater.

Having this awareness makes life much easier. It provides comfort through the storms. The old me would've panicked at the thought of losing my job. I felt physically and emotionally sick because I didn't want to have to go through it, knowing my stability and comfort level were going to be shaken. Fortunately, my faith had grown over the years.

It was around the summer of 2012 when I began writing in a journal. I received a small notebook from my church's women's retreat and decided to write down my thoughts and feelings to the Lord. I didn't write frequently in the beginning of my journaling, only when I felt significantly overwhelmed. It was during times of uncertainty, I'd write to the Lord about how I knew I could trust Him and asked forgiveness for any disbelief and disobedience.

It was also during this time where I continued to pray for His will to be done. One of the lessons I learned at this point in my life was to trust in God's will, not my own. I started to learn how to let go of the burdens I carried and worries of an uncertain future.

Hope was in sight. A blessing had been revealed through my distress. I remembered I had a 401k plan from which I could withdraw some money. It would provide stable income for a while, which lessened the stress of having to leave my job. I was at ease but had to consider my living arrangement. The lease for my apartment would be up in a few months, and they required a two month notice if I was going to vacate. I had to make a hasty decision, and time was running out.

I submitted a notice to my employer shortly before my daytime class started. I had to make many swift and difficult decisions without knowing what to do. I spent much time in prayer because I felt lost. I didn't know where I was going to live when November came around, but I knew God had a plan for me.

Damon and I had been a part of a small, Bible teaching church family since 2008. Through the most difficult times, they were there for us. We were shown great love and care. I learned a great deal about who God is through His Word. Additionally, I learned how to grow into deeper relationship with my Creator over the span of nine years as a member of this church.

I turned to our church family for help. As I expressed concern about where Damon and I were going to live, my pastor's wife offered their home to us. Their hospitality was a blessing, and I don't know if I could ever repay them.

When I reflect on all the things God has done, tears come flowing down with an inexpressible joy. It's difficult to include all instances where God blessed us and displayed His kindness, mercy, and love, even in my unfaithfulness. The joy of the Lord cannot be shaken by trials and tribulations.

The devil no longer has a hold on my life. Even though there are times where it feels like I'm sinking into the pit of despair and hope is lost, the truth of God will always prevail. He lifts me back up and restores my soul.

One of the greatest challenges I faced was furthering my education. It was tough trying to balance multiple responsibilities, but I never gave up. I worked hard to move up out of my previous circumstances. Nothing was going to stop me from proving I can do anything through Christ's strength, even though there were times I felt like giving up.

Obtaining a bachelor of arts degree was a great accomplishment. I majored in social work and minored in sociology because of my desire to help others in need. I attended the graduation ceremony in May 2013, with the company of a few family members. It felt surreal being called up to the stage by name, followed by the words *Cum Laude Honors*.

I officially graduated in July 2013 after completing my final credits and received my diploma. Following graduation, I studied to become a Certified Social Worker (CSW). While this caused great deal of anxiety, I passed the state and national exams, relying solely on the Lord's guidance. He held my hand throughout this journey, leading me through times of uncertainty and doubt. After five years of schooling, it was now time to see what I was made of.

Throughout the spring and summer, I sent my resume out to various agencies in Wisconsin. Most of them were in the southeast region, but if the job seemed worthwhile, I'd also apply further away. I attended a handful of interviews, but due to lack of experience, they didn't hire me. I was disappointed but knew it wasn't meant to be. I had to wait for God's timing and His will to be done.

Searching for employment was exhausting. I was discouraged, believing no agency was going to hire me. Then one day, I received a call. The director of an agency serving persons who had developmental disabilities in Madison requested to schedule an interview. We discussed the fact that the commute would be two hours away. I told her I'd consider relocating if the job was worthwhile.

The position I applied for provided residential case management services in Dane County. After some contemplation, I decided to take the job. My first job in the field of social work began in July 2013.

Deep down, I hoped for a big change. Throughout my life, I often wanted to run from my problems, as if to escape them. Unfortunately, problems don't go away if you never learn to resolve them. I looked forward to the upcoming change but didn't realize how much it'd affect me. I was going to be a few hours away from my comfort zone, leaving behind my support system—family, friends, and church.

Once I settled into the new job, I began searching for an apartment and a private school for Damon. The difficult part was having to choose a school first. I always felt strongly about keeping Damon in a small Christian school. The primary focus was to raise him up in the Lord not only at home, but at school as well. I decided it'd be easier to locate a school closer to my employer, in order to broaden my apartment search.

The Lord led us to a Lutheran school near my employer, which piqued my interest. I began the enrollment process for Damon to start second grade in the coming year. My next goal was to find an apartment outside the city of Madison. After some discussion with coworkers who were more familiar with the area, I decided to move to a small village on the outskirts of Madison in September 2013. The daily commute prior to the move totaled four hours a day: two hours to work and two hours home.

I made trips to the gas station about four times a week to fill my tank. At close to $4.00 a gallon, I wasn't able to save any money. My paychecks went to gas and bills. Thankfully, my dear friends at church helped provide a security deposit for us. Additionally, my employer arranged a short term stay in a spare room during the week to save time and gas.

Shortly after the move, feelings of isolation kicked in. I was also homesick. I didn't know anyone in the area and couldn't drive back to my hometown any time I felt like it. Damon and I spent a lot of time keeping busy outside. We went on walks around the neighborhood, spent time by the lake, and kept an eye out for various activities in the city.

It wasn't easy trying to enjoy life without friends or family nearby. Adjusting to our new surroundings proved difficult. It was almost like a culture shock. I learned a lot about others' ideologies, lifestyles, and worldviews. Looking back now, I learned to love others more, regardless of our differences. At work, we all seemed to share in the same passion to help others who were vulnerable and required advocacy.

With no one to help keep me in line and encourage me in the Lord, I started to back slide and fell into sin. The Holy Spirit convicted me of my sinfulness, but oftentimes, I didn't care. I was upset for being left alone. There was no one to hold me accountable but myself. It wasn't God's fault. I made the decision to look for work elsewhere, hoping to escape from my problems.

My spiritual wellbeing diminished as shame and guilt led to a reduction in my prayer life. This resulted in feeling separated from God. I didn't sense His presence like I did in other situations.

To ease my loneliness, I decided to try online dating again. I've had several unsuccessful experiences with online dating in my time yet always continued to search, hoping there was someone out there for me. While my main intention this time was to make new friends, I ended up meeting men who wanted more. I hadn't yet grasped that in the world around me, people were a little *too* casual in their dating habits. Even if people say they're looking for friendship, it seems "friends with benefits" is almost expected. Maybe I'm old fashioned, but friendship to me doesn't come with "sexual benefits."

Through a dating site, I met a man named Steve, who asked me out for a drink. We got along okay, and he eventually made it clear he liked me. I wasn't interested in having a relationship from the beginning but wanted to remain friends. After going out a few times, we ended up having intercourse. I was intoxicated at the time and hadn't yet learned going out to drink with a stranger is *never* a good idea. I ended up cutting communication with him because I was frustrated. I allowed it to happen, despite my wishes. The word *no* or any variation of it doesn't seem to deter a lot of men in this day and age. Now don't get me wrong, there are several men out there who remain respectful to women, and I commend them for this wonderful quality. However, many will be relentless in their pursuit of scoring with a woman they want.

According to what I've seen and experienced, those kinds of men particularly prey on vulnerable women with low self esteem. I admit, my self esteem needed a lot of work. It took several more years to change my self hatred into self acceptance. It wouldn't be until much later on where I took a passage from 2 Timothy to heart in this area of my life.

> But mark this: There will be terrible times in the last days. People will be lovers of themselves, lovers of money, boastful, proud, abusive, disobedient to their parents, ungrateful, unholy, without love, unforgiving, slanderous, without self control, brutal, not lovers of the good, treacherous, rash, conceited, lovers of pleasure rather than lovers of God, having a form of godliness but denying its power. Have nothing to do with such people. They are the kind who worm their way into homes and gain control over gullible women, who are loaded down with sins and are swayed by all kinds of evil desires, always learning but never able to come to a knowledge of the truth. They are men of depraved minds, who, as far as the faith is concerned, are rejected. (2 Tim. 3:1–8 NIV)

Sadly, I continued to give in to men's sexual advances throughout the course of my learning journey. It was a vicious cycle I never seemed to escape for about four more years, until I finally said enough is enough. It took having the courage to report a sexual assault to open my eyes of the dangers of casual dating. At that point, I cut online dating for good. You'll read about the assault in a later chapter.

Back to the story. Steve had a friend named Curt who frequented the local bars where Steve and I hung out. It was a tiny village with not much to do, so people went to the bars to socialize. Curt apparently became interested and approached me. He was a bit older, which led me to assume he'd have a more mature personality than what I was accustomed to. Deep down, I knew this was a bad idea. I ignored red flags as usual and allowed him into my life. I'm not sure why I continued to see him. Why haven't I learned my lesson yet? The only explanation I can think of is that it could have been my way of trying to fill an emptiness that no man could truly fill. If there's one bit of advice I could give, it'd be to always trust your intuition. If you notice bright red flags, please run and don't look back.

Curt's behavior changed after a little while. It seemed like he was trying to take control of me. He came over to my apartment, acting like he owned the place. We hadn't known each other long, so his behaviors became concerning. He asked if he could move a few things into my storage locker located in the basement of the apartment building. I told him it'd be fine. He asked Damon to help him move the items from his truck. Unfortunately, I wasn't paying attention to the move. I happened to go to the basement days later to retrieve something from storage and saw it was full of Curt's belongings. It was almost like he moved in!

The issues progressed. He began to insult and belittle me. I recall one time he made me cry and felt no remorse. I attempted to share my written testimony with him but he wasn't interested. This validated the fact he didn't care about me as a person. I was fed up. I told him I was going to put his belongings outside, and he could come pick them up. Curt thought I wouldn't be able to do it without him since there were some heavier boxes. He told me to wait for him, but that didn't stop me. God has a way of making this tiny person possess super human strength when necessary. I laid his things out on the snow covered parking lot next to the back door, including the heavy, bulky items.

Curt was then cut out of my life. I refused to allow anyone to control me. I took pride in being a strong, independent woman, and no one was going to take it from me. Now don't get me wrong, I'm highly dependent on Jehovah Jireh ("The Lord who provides") to take care of all my needs. Nevertheless, I cannot allow someone to steal my independence as a means to control me.

While residing in Dane county, I began to journal about my fall into sin and begged the Lord to forgive me and lead me back into His righteous path. I expressed feelings of pain and sorrow and turned them into prayers. Something occurred in the midst of my journaling. God always speaks to His children, either through His Word, repetitious messages, or sometimes through music. There were times I cried out to Him with Christian music playing in the background. Then all of a sudden, the right song with the right lyrics play as His response to me.

A song happened to come on the radio confirming that God won't forsake me. His message to me was I knew what I needed to do. I had to get rid of that intentional sin. I didn't recognize the purpose of the suffering I experienced but knew it'd come in time. I'll always hold on to El Shaddai's ("God Almighty") promise that He'll never leave me or forsake me. In the days I cried out to Him in desperation, I know He heard me. The Word tells me so. I'll share a few encouraging Bible verses:

> This is the confidence we have in approaching God: that if we ask anything according to his will, he hears us. (1 John 5:14 NIV)

> The eyes of the Lord are on the righteous, and His ears are attentive to their cry. The righteous cry out, and the Lord hears them; He delivers them from all their troubles. The Lord is close to the brokenhearted and saves those who are crushed in spirit. The righteous person may have many

troubles, but the Lord delivers him from them all. (Psa. 34:15–19)

When I place God first in my life, I'm not anxious or depressed. I feel peace, joy, and contentment, knowing His will is greater and all things will work out for His glory. The process of coming back to God and being faithful to His Word is difficult but not impossible.

5
SINFUL DESIRES LEAD TO UNDESIREABLE OUTCOMES

While I continued to strive in the task of reducing sinful behaviors, temptation continued to rule in areas I felt weakest. Throughout the fall and winter season of 2013–2014, I journaled about how I was unable to feel the Lord's presence. I wasn't reading the Word, which would've provided encouragement and direction. The good news is, there's always hope when you turn to God for help in times of desperation. You just have to be willing to listen.

In the midst of struggling with fleshly desires and trying to get right with God again, I made yet another unwise decision to search for companionship online. Not much time has passed since I had cut Curt out of the picture. My heart's desire was to find a Christian man to share common beliefs with, but he was hard to come by. Oftentimes, my dates told me they're Christian, but their lives reflected the opposite. Here's another example.

I exchanged messages with a seemingly nice man named Charles, and we eventually met face to face. I mentioned I was interested in having a relationship with a Christian man but am open to friendship with anyone. His response to my statement wasn't clear, but he ended up saying he was a Christian. But Charles was far from being a Christian, as I'd later realized. Things moved pretty quickly between us as we decided to get into a relationship.

In March 2014, I decided to figure out a method of birth control. I was hesitant because I received a birth control injection immediately after Damon's birth. After a few years passed taking the injection, I experienced side effects of hair loss and weight gain. I also stopped getting my period. This wasn't natural. I decided to discontinue the shot and hadn't looked into any other options for birth control until my relationship with Charles. My doctor at the time recommended an IUD. She explained it wouldn't enter the bloodstream, so I wouldn't experience those same side effects as the injection. Little did I know the insertion of this IUD would cause a bit of Post Traumatic Stress Disorder (PTSD).

Choosing to date Charles resulted in several negative consequences. I was in an unhealthy relationship with a man who wasn't a Christian. The primary issue was our values didn't align, which caused me to fall into sexual sin. Placing man and fleshly desires before God leads to negative consequences. As I contemplated a major decision regarding birth control, Charles had no interest in supporting me through it. When we discussed attending the appointment together, he backed out shortly before the scheduled visit.

Throughout our relationship, I was expected to support him in his hobbies and interests. His world revolved around his hobby: archery. I attended target practice and competitions. If I commented about it being just a hobby, he got angry. He was also into MMA fights on television. I could never bring myself to watch it because I'd become sensitive to violence. We had nothing in common. He didn't support anything I was interested in. Our differences became obvious, which resulted in frequent arguments. Even though I was in a relationship, I felt completely rejected and alone.

I headed to the IUD appointment on my own. It'd be an understatement to say this was an unpleasant experience. I learned the doctor performing the procedure was a student, who was observed by a trained professional. They reviewed important information as the procedure began. If the IUD was placed inside my body incorrectly, there could be severe consequences. Additionally, if I experienced any discharge the following day, I was instructed to call the doctor right away.

The procedure was a nightmare. I wasn't prepared for the excruciating pain. I always assumed my pain tolerance was high. I wailed loudly as I was being dilated and he inserted the device into my vagina. The professional held my hand tightly. I felt terribly violated. The emotional effects following the procedure were devastating. After arriving home, I wanted to go to bed. I couldn't stop crying. It was more like loud, agonized sobbing. Tears flowed, and the feeling of discomfort was overwhelming. Poor Damon came in my bedroom and asked what was wrong. I told him I didn't feel good.

At eight years old, he knew exactly how to comfort his mom. He grabbed a box of tissues; a glass of water, and my teddy bear I've had since I was a toddler. I know it sounds silly, but oftentimes when I'm in pain, I grab my bear and hold it, even into adulthood. I called my doctor's office the next day in panic, as I saw what looked like discharge on my underwear. The nurse assured me it was normal and I'd be okay, but if it were to continue, I should call her back. It took a few days to recover physically, but the emotional effects continued, even into my work day as I sat at my desk. I had difficulty concentrating and held in the tears as they desperately wanted to come out. Thankfully, my colleagues were caring and empathetic.

My relationship with Charles ended not long after the procedure. I was devastated. I worked hard to build our relationship and make him happy. Unfortunately, the feeling wasn't mutual. There were red flags and warning signs throughout our time together. As usual, I ignored them thinking he had potential to change if only I prayed hard enough for it.

When it seems like our prayers aren't answered, we have to look deep within to see what our true intentions are. Are we asking for something to gratify the fleshly nature, or are we praying for God's will, so He might receive the glory? Do we ask with humble hearts, truly desiring God's outcome rather than our own? Father knows best, and I believe sometimes we don't get what we ask for because it isn't in our best interest. What we're asking for could potentially do more harm than good. That harm will likely outweigh the pain we feel when we don't get our way, but we'll get over it. Pain is temporary. What I've learned in the healing process of each failed relationship is simple. I'll word it in the way a humorous friend of mine once said, "Look at it this way, you dodged a bullet!"

I was now becoming increasingly emotional and hyper sensitive. After the breakup, I continued to pray God would change Charles's heart and mind, so we could be restored. I knew my sinfulness led me to this dark place. I continued to break my vow to the Lord, the vow that I'd no longer give in to sexual temptation. I always seemed to fail and felt nothing but shame.

Ever since I became a believer, my heart's desire was to find a good Christian husband. My church did a fine job teaching what a godly marriage looks like and led by example. After going through many breakups with ungodly men, I prayed the Lord would take my desire away. It appeared there were no genuine Christian men in my generation. I wanted to be content as a single person for the rest of my life. I couldn't stand the pain of heartbreak. I no longer wanted to feel rejected, let down, depressed, or anxious about any relationship. It often led me to resent the person who caused those feelings. God began to show me I had to forgive those who inflicted great pain.

A few months later, I went to a follow up appointment with my primary doctor. I explained to the nurse how emotional I've been as a result of the IUD. There were many stressful factors, which could've played a role in my severe depression. I was recovering from a broken relationship, I felt homesick, I had several uncomfortable procedures done at the dentist office over a span of three months, and I worked at an extremely stressful job.

My doctor administered a depression assessment. I was familiar with this assessment in my experience as a social worker. I knew I was going to score somewhat high. She told me she was concerned about my reaction to the IUD, stating it wasn't normal. She believed I might have PTSD.

Any time a thought or visualization entered my mind about the IUD experience I quickly repressed them.

I displayed several symptoms of depression: feelings of sadness and not understanding why, random bouts of crying, having little motivation to do things I typically enjoyed, and so on. Her recommendation was to try an antidepressant. She firmly believed I had "chemical imbalances" in my brain. I was hesitant to try medication, but she insisted I give it a try and wrote out a prescription.

I decided to call my pastor for advice. He worked as a pharmacist, and I trusted his input. After receiving reassurance, I decided to try the medication. Though the side effects were uncomfortable, I noticed improvement in my mood. It was a great feeling, but there was a downside. Something new and quite concerning had developed—involuntary movements in my fingers. I talked with a colleague about the side effect, and she encouraged me to talk to my doctor about stopping the antidepressant. Someone on her caseload experienced involuntary movements on the same medication, and they found out too late it was irreversible. I took it upon myself to stop immediately.

During another follow up visit, my doctor prescribed a different antidepressant, but the same side effect occurred and this one didn't improve my mood. I decided to give up on medications because the benefits didn't seem to outweigh the risks.

I hadn't even lived in Madison for one year and desperately wanted to go back home. I knew I had to rely on the Lord to get me through this. I prayed regularly, requesting a change in my circumstances. I drove to the lake to journal my thoughts, feelings, and prayers to the Lord. I praised Him through my suffering with a new appreciation. I reflected on where I came from, and what I've made it through. This led to a greater understanding that whatever happens in life, the will of God will always benefit His children. My trust in Him began to increase throughout this distressing time.

I waited for things to change, not knowing exactly what I was waiting for. Peace filled my heart as I went out to meet with the Lord in the beauty of His creation. I began to recognize His presence in the wind and looked to the heavens where He resides. My favorite part in all creation are the skies and the clouds. I can't help being distracted as my eyes gaze upward to the beautiful colors of the sunrise and sunset. Music also played a huge role in bringing comfort during this stormy season of my life. Oftentimes, I listened to the local Christian radio station or played Christian music on my playlist to calm my racing heart. The messages and lyrics in the various songs I heard reaffirmed God's love and care for me. I shed many tears as I replayed special songs to help me cope through the heartbreak.

As my relationship with the Lord grew, I listened for His still, small voice. He desired for me to sit with Him and spend more time with Him. He was the calm in the storm, even in the midst of my brokenness. He assured me everything would be fine as I sat with Him in nature. Peace and quiet were something I started to crave. It was here where I learned my sensitivity was a result of having the Holy Spirit within, having a heart like God's. Years before, I prayed my heart would be changed, in order to have a heart more like God's. Little did I know how much of a difference it'd make and how it'd affect me.

This Bible verse makes a great prayer while developing a deeper relationship with the Lord: "Create in me a pure heart, O God, and renew a steadfast spirit within me. Do not cast me from your presence or take your Holy Spirit from me. Restore to me the joy of your salvation and grant me a willing spirit, to sustain me" (Psa. 51:10–12 NIV).

I was now learning how to wait patiently on the Lord. In the past, I attempted to do it all on my own. I made hasty decisions, which resulted in poor outcomes. I rarely thought things through. I especially didn't pray about them, either. Following God's deliverance, I noticed a difference between times I made hasty decisions and times I prayed that God's will would be done. I still struggled with complete surrender to His will, as I was yet a new believer. But as time went on,

I discovered His plans were always greater than what I had in mind. My trust increased yet again.

It didn't take long for God to give me a sign. It was around September 2014 when I received a call from an employer. She saw my resume online and requested an interview. It sounded promising, and the salary was about the same. The best part was the job was closer to home. I certainly knew if it was God's divine plan, I'd get the job. The interview was a success. Surprisingly, I wasn't anxious and had self confidence. The HR representative told me she liked my personality, and I was offered the job. This meant we'd be moving yet again.

I became familiar with instability throughout my adult years, having no direction. Damon became accustomed to changes throughout his young life as well. I felt bad about the number of times he had to switch schools. It was hard for him to make new friends and leave the old ones behind. I hoped and prayed for stability. The two of us were relieved to come back home. We moved in with my parents in order to save money for an apartment. We went to our old church for Sunday service, and I found out they had been praying for us to return. It was a joy to know others were thinking about us and praying for us. Oh, to be surrounded by familiar faces in a familiar environment!

My new job was in family care as a case manager. It began with extensive training, as I was required to become a certified long term care functional screener. Once training was complete, my caseload significantly increased to around eighty members. The daily pressure and demands led me to second guess working for this agency. How can one person competently and effectively support eighty members in a forty hour work week?

I was given the option to work from home because the company provided laptops and cell phones. There are some advantages and disadvantages working from home. The primary advantage was the ability to work in a peaceful environment without interruption from coworkers. The primary disadvantage was giving into the temptation to work beyond business hours, oftentimes without taking a break. It must be my strong work ethic, but I was determined to keep up with the demands and case notes. It seemed never ending.

Of course, putting a lot of pressure on myself negatively affected my health. In college, they stressed the importance of self care for social workers, due to the high risk of burnout. I always thought, "There's no time for self care when I have a lot to do!" The truth is, you must make time. My employer had a high turnover rate, similar to my previous job. It didn't take long to realize this wasn't a good fit. The burden was too overwhelming. I wondered if all social service jobs were going to be like this.

6

STANDING FIRM IN FAITH OVERCOMES HARDSHIPS

Within a few months, I located an apartment in Mount Pleasant, Wisconsin, and we moved in December 2014. After settling in, I began to seek out other employment options. I submitted resumes and cover letters like there was no tomorrow, trusting in the Lord to help me.

I wasn't writing in my journal as much or spending time reading God's Word, which meant I continued to learn hard lessons. I proceeded to date, hoping to find a husband. It wouldn't be until much later that I finally decided to stop searching in the wrong places. Unfortunately, at this time, I didn't think too much of it. I wondered why certain people were placed in my path. Being rejected and used by several men caused a great deal of pain. I was sick of the dating game because it affected my self esteem. One could understand if I turned out to be a so called "man hater," which was the case around my mid twenties.

Thankfully, God taught me how to forgive and let go of the pain people caused me. I was in my early thirties when I no longer allowed bitterness and hatred to take over. Healing still had to take place, and it took time, but letting go felt much better. God places people in our path to teach us something. Whether the experiences are positive or negative, we learn from them, regardless.

The Lord showed me I should rather act in love, not under impulse. When I easily want to give up on others, God reminds me to hold on and be patient. The Bible reminds me where to place my trust:

> Be still, and know that I am God. (Psa. 46:10 NIV)

> It is better to take refuge in the Lord than to trust in humans. (Psa. 118:8 NIV)

> The Lord himself goes before you and will be with you; he will never leave you nor forsake you. Do not be afraid; do not be discouraged. (Deut. 31:8 NIV)

Jesus confirmed in John 16:33 that we'll experience trouble in this life. People hurt us and let us down because we all inherently struggle with sin, but our Lord, who is without sin, will never let us down. He is fully trustworthy and reliable. He gently speaks the truth to us for our own good through His Word.

In my continual disobedience, I turned to the world to fill the emptiness inside, which resulted in heartache and pain. Nonetheless, Jehovah Rapha ("The Lord who heals") faithfully came to heal and restore my soul time and time again. I strongly relate to Paul's explanation of his struggle with sin:

> We know that the law is spiritual; but I am unspiritual, sold as a slave to sin. I do not understand what I do. For what I want to do I do not do, but what I hate I do. And if I do what I do not want to do, I agree that the law is good. As it is, it is no longer I myself who do it, but it is sin living in me. For I know that good itself does not dwell in me, that is, in my sinful nature. For I have the desire to do what is good, but I cannot carry it out. For I do not do the good I want to do, but the evil I do not want to do—this I keep on doing. Now if I do what I do not want to do, it is no longer I who do it, but it is sin living in me that does it. So, I find this law at work: Although I want to do good, evil is right there with me. For in my inner being I delight in God's law; but I see another law at work in me, waging war against the law of my mind and making me a prisoner of the law of sin at work within me. What a

wretched man I am! Who will rescue me from this body that is subject to death? Thanks be to God, who delivers me through Jesus Christ our Lord! (Rom. 7:14–25 NIV)

My employment search came to an end in April 2015. I accepted an offer from a skilled nursing facility as a social service case manager. It was a temporary assignment covering two maternity leaves consecutively. The decision was risky because I had a permanent job in place, but I was willing to take a leap of faith. Deep down, I knew it'd help me obtain the experience I needed for what I thought was my dream job: working in a long term care setting with an elderly population.

My position began by covering the first three month maternity leave in the rehabilitation unit. Within that time frame, one of the three social workers put in a notice of resignation. She covered one of the long term care units on the other side of the facility. I was offered her position and accepted. I was ecstatic the Lord answered my prayer for a permanent position, especially for the type of work I wanted to do.

The only thing is, something didn't quite sit right. I couldn't figure out what it was at the time. Residents, their family members, and my colleagues revealed things I took into consideration. I found out I was the unit's fifth social worker in three years. I was told my predecessor always walked around looking stressed out or high strung. People questioned, "Why is there a high turnover in social workers?" I kept this concerning information in mind.

Reasons for the high turnover eventually came to light. Training for the long term care unit was entirely inadequate, and the supervisor was unsupportive. My unit was often filled with tension and division. I regretted accepting the offer. I wondered if I made the right decision and couldn't help but feel disappointed. Eventually, stress related symptoms manifested inside. I knew what was coming. The longer I worked in the field of social work, the more I recognized an increased risk of developing anxiety and depression, especially if I worked with individuals who had severe mental health issues.

In the past, I only experienced Seasonal Affective Disorder from the end of winter into early spring. Once the weather warmed up, I walked daily and occasionally jogged to burn off stress. Spending time outside in the sun helped me significantly. However, a new issue developed. When summer came to an end, I became anxious, knowing I wouldn't be able to spend as much time in the sun and burn off the stress. I wasn't physically active during the winter season. Cold weather and snow deter me from going outdoors, and I couldn't afford a gym membership.

Depression and anxiety worsened under stress, and typically my stress was work related. The worst part was when I left one job for another. I felt great compassion for my clients, and many of them loved me. Social workers are sometimes the only person a client can trust. Their loved ones either abandon them or live too far away to help. Saying goodbye was always hard.

There were stress related factors outside of work as well. Being a single parent is one of the toughest jobs out there. I raised Damon alone since birth, and the financial obligations can be overwhelming. Moving also contributes to stress because you have to update your change of address, potentially switch schools, and haul your belongings from one place to another. One person can only tolerate so much in their life. I wanted to reevaluate my career path. Was social work really for me?

Toward the end of October 2015, I came across a notice at work from the infection control nurse. Employees were required to get the flu shot and if proof was not received by November 20, you weren't allowed to come into work until you provided the proof. The only exception was a doctor's note confirming an allergy to the injection. This concerned me because my supervisor told me the flu shot wasn't mandatory when I was hired. I was reluctant to speak to her because communication with her was often vague and unclear. I told her this was the first time I heard about the flu shot being mandatory, and I had no intention of receiving the injection.

I went to the Infection Control nurse to find out what the policy specifically entailed, as requested by my supervisor. There were only two options. Either you get the flu shot or provide a doctor's note saying you are allergic to it. During the conversation, I attempted to explain my personal reasons for discontinuing the shot years ago. My primary concern was I tend to be sensitive to side effects. Also, after doing research, I didn't want to have those ingredients injected into my body. When I attempted to discuss options, she refused to listen. At the time, I was tempted to give in and get it done. There were designated times posted for employees to receive the shot on campus. I figured I was going to go on the next available date.

My nights were spent with anxious thoughts as well as anger. I thought, *Why should I be forced to do something I feel strongly against? It's appalling that this is a condition of employment, especially when I saw the research about how ineffective it can be, as well as the negative side effects that could occur.* The worst part was I had little time to get things figured out. I went above my supervisor by sending an email, explaining the situation and to inquire about other options for employment. Payroll and job placement were through an outside provider. Shortly after, my supervisor returned to offer a suggestion of scheduling an appointment with my doctor to see if I could acquire a note and go from there. I didn't have a primary physician at the time, so I scheduled an appointment with a new doctor. The earliest available appointment was one week prior to the November 20 deadline.

During the visit, the doctor refused to write a note. I wasn't surprised. I decided to bring up how I've been feeling increased anxiety and depression. Per protocol, she recommended medication. I described the negative outcomes from previous antidepressants. She wrote a prescription for a different medication and told me to think about it. I called my pastor again for reassurance and, after speaking to him, decided to try the antidepressant.

The next day I went into work feeling tremendously anxious. I knew I had to turn in my notice, and the deadline was exactly one week away. I concluded my notice, stating I wouldn't get the flu shot. My supervisor was surprised when I handed it to her. She asked if I wanted to give more than a week's notice. I told her with the deadline I had no choice. I wasn't prepared for this unexpected turn of events. The facility dropped the ball in regard to properly notifying me about the flu shot being a condition of employment. I was about to lose my job. As I explained earlier, the toughest part of being a social worker is saying goodbye to those on your caseload. I held back many tears as I said my goodbyes, but some of the residents were unable to hold in theirs.

At this point I decided I didn't want to be a social worker anymore. There was an overwhelming sense of emotional exhaustion, sadness, and fear. I had enough of being pushed and pulled in all different directions—in other words I was experiencing burnout. Around the time I left the job, my health took a turn for the worse. For the first time ever, I experienced a few panic attacks, though I didn't realize it at first. I wondered what was wrong with me and concluded it could be a combination of starting the new medication and the stress at work.

There were several indications, which led to the panic attack and anxiety episodes. My breathing was off, my heart rate was unusually rapid, I felt sick to my stomach, and I had no appetite, I was wide awake at night, I cried often, my head felt cloudy, I was restless, and surprisingly I thought I wanted to die. People began to notice this decline in my health and prayed prayers for healing and employment on my behalf and for our needs to be met.

I decided to go out into nature again to meet with the Lord. He led me to a more isolated place that I came across on a walk with a relative. I sat there hoping to feel His presence and peace, desiring to listen to whatever it was He would say to me. I brought my journal and wrote down what I heard. I desired to hear that still, small voice. The following is taken from a journal entry. The Lord's response is italicized:

> 11/20/15. I'm not to worry. I'm being prepared for something greater but am not to know what just yet. I am stronger than I think. Being stubborn isn't necessarily a bad thing, it helps me to stand up for what I believe and for what's right. God is here with me. He'll provide as He always has. Greater things are to come, don't forget this. His peace will cover me. Rest and take care of myself. Damon and I have a special purpose. We are loved by Him and others. The Lord is giving me these words: *"You were homeless, you were hungry, and you attempted to end your life. Who kept you protected? Who fed you? Who clothed you? Who saved you? Who gave you purpose? Who gave you life? I can do all things. I can heal you from your sickness. I can provide all your needs. I'll care for you forever. Do not worry, do not fear, and last of all, do not cry. I am your helper."*

There's always an unexplainable sense of comfort when the Lord speaks to you. Sometimes when I read my journal entries long after their written, I'm surprised to see what I've overcome and how God has helped me through it. I see answered prayers following my emotional pleas for help. Looking back at His faithfulness inevitably increases my faith and trust in Him.

My entries fluctuated between anger at how God allows bad things to happen to me and cries for Him to rescue me from despair. I'd complain that He doesn't hear me or care about what I'm going through. They're always followed by praises to God that He did, in fact, hear me, He did respond, and my joy was restored. I realize I shouldn't direct my anger at Him. If you read through the book of Psalms, it has a similar pattern. An elder once told me the book of Psalms is great for depression.

It's hard to see how anything could get you through the storm when you're in it, but once the storm is over, you can look back and remember suffering isn't permanent. You made it through somehow. God always gives His children hope. I continue to overcome obstacles that'll inevitably come my way because I know God is with me and He is for me.

> I have learned to be content whatever the circumstances. I know what it is to be in need, and I know what it is to have plenty. I have learned the secret of being content in any and every situation, whether well fed or hungry, whether living in plenty or in want. I can do all this through him who gives me strength. (Phil. 4:11–13 NIV)

I recuperated after a few days and continued searching for employment. The time off was necessary for me to start thinking straight again. It also helped me to focus on reading the Bible more. When times are good, I tend to put reading God's Word on the backburner. When tough times come, I'm not adequately prepared to handle them because His Word is what provides direction and assurance. As I read the Bible again, a sense of peace entered. My previous tendencies would be to go off and do things on my own without seeking counsel from the Almighty. All He wants is for me to just breathe and trust in Him.

We were blessed as we experienced love from those around us. Our church family took turns bringing dinner a few days a week. Friends called to see how I was doing. My parents offered their home to us as I knew I wouldn't be able to afford to pay both bills and rent. I knew I was sacrificing a higher income, which came with the social work degree, but my mental health was more valuable to me than money. I searched for jobs related to manufacturing, where I was most experienced outside of the degree. The following month, in December 2015, I received an offer for an electrical assembly position. The pay was far less than what I was accustomed to, but it didn't matter. My health was far more important. I was relieved to be responsible for parts and not people. I was grateful to be able to pay my bills.

My church family became concerned about my health following the nursing home job and offered to pay for a Christian counselor. It was difficult for me to accept the offer, but I felt it was something God wanted me to do to help me heal. I also needed to learn how to cope and deal with my issues. I arranged to see her twice a month and found it helpful after what seemed like a slow start.

My new job was easy, and I got to meet new people. While things in life went on as usual, I was unaware of another traumatic event heading my way. This time, it'd involve a new coworker, named Brad who was hired shortly after me. For some reason, he'd often go out of his way to talk to me. I thought it was strange because we didn't work in the same area. He was short in stature, around my height, and presented himself as incredibly smug. There was a weird vibe about him, but I ignored it. It's *never* good to ignore your intuition. You'll see why.

7

RELY ON THE LORD TO PERSEVERE AGAINST EVIL

It was early January 2016 when a coworker stopped and asked if I was married or currently "on the market." I joked with her saying, "I'm practically always single." She was about to walk away, when all of a sudden, she turned and said, "My friend likes you." I had a feeling I knew who it was but didn't think anything of it because I wasn't interested in him. Not long after the conversation, Brad grew more persistent. It was time to clock out, and we all headed to our cars. It snowed that day, so we had to clean off our cars. As I brushed the snow off my windows, Brad walked up to my car. He said he wanted to hang out and gave me his number. Since I wasn't interested in going out with him, I tried to make an excuse. His persistence continued.

LIFE LESSON

He said he came from another state and didn't know anyone in the area, which led me to feel bad for him. That weird vibe remained as I reluctantly invited him to a friend's birthday party the following weekend. I later texted him my number, in order to plan the details for the birthday party. I should've known better from previous mistakes not to freely give out my number. There were two instances in the past where I changed my phone number due to an excessive amount of unwanted calls from a few men who refused to take no for an answer. The first occurred around 2006 and the second around 2011.

I prefer to give people the benefit of a doubt, but it's best to take proper precautions. When it comes to strangers, you never know the type of people you're dealing with. After receiving my text, he began to send messages at an unusual rate. It made me uncomfortable, but I continued to respond, keeping my responses brief.

Brad insisted on driving the night of the birthday party. I would've preferred to drive myself, but assumed I'd be safe since we worked together. I also planned on going home alone, but that wasn't Brad's intention. The group of us celebrating my friend's birthday went to a few local bars in downtown Kenosha. It was getting late, and I was ready to leave.

I know my limit when it comes to drinking alcohol. I stuck to my limit that night as usual. I wanted to use the restroom before we left. When I came out, the bartender brought out a few shots. I didn't plan on having any shots and declined the offer, but Brad and the bartender insisted. Feeling pressured, I took it. Immediately, I felt strange like I wanted to pass out. My head became cloudy, and it felt like I was hit by a ton of bricks. I never experienced this sensation after a drink. I quickly said my goodbyes because all I could think about was going to bed to pass out.

As Brad pulled up to the front entrance of my apartment complex, he asked if I wanted company. I told him I didn't want to do anything. He claimed nothing was going to happen. He just wanted somewhere to crash, so he didn't have to drive. At the moment, my primary concern was getting to bed. I decided to allow him in. I had difficulty staying awake as a result of whatever was in that shot. Brad decided to climb into bed with me and ended up committing sexual assault by rape. I told him I wasn't on birth control, and he told me not to worry because he couldn't have children. I repeated I didn't want to do anything with him, but he didn't stop.

I was physically unable to stop him and felt completely numb. I couldn't understand what was occurring because my mindset was altered. I couldn't do anything about what was taking place. After the rape, I stopped responding to his text messages. I disregarded his approaches at work. He acted in total ignorance, as if nothing was wrong.

My birthday happened to be in the middle of the following week. I was at work when my team lead walked up with a bouquet of flowers. I assumed it was from the company. When I looked at the card, there was a picture of a four leaf clover on it. I immediately felt nauseated because I knew it was from Brad. He always bragged about being Irish. I gave the flowers away to coworkers. I wanted nothing to do with them.

When I saw my counselor on our next visit, she knew something was wrong. There was an expression in my face, which gave it away. I told her everything. She told me I had her full support and strongly suggested I file a police report on Brad for sexual assault. I didn't realize I had been sexually assaulted because my mind led me to believe it was partly my fault. I allowed it to happen. She reminded me I didn't consent to having sex. Additionally, my pastor who worked as a pharmacist told me, based on the symptoms, it sounded like I was given a date rape drug. It's true; it wasn't my fault it happened.

It was tough gathering enough courage to file the report, but I went to the police station anyway. I felt empowered standing up for myself, knowing my decision could prevent someone else from going through the same thing. All I had was his first name and a phone number. The police later looked him up and contacted him to get his side of the story. Unfortunately, I decided not to press charges. I was advised to tell Brad to stop texting me, to not approach my car, and to stop walking past my work bench. If he continued with those behaviors, I could place a restraining order for harassment. Once I sent the warning via text message, he immediately stopped communicating with me. I wondered if this was something familiar to him.

After eventually learning his last name, I decided to look up his public records and found a disturbing criminal history. There were mug shots taken from various arrests, which confirmed it was the same person who assaulted me. I also came across a news article from the state he claimed he was from, regarding the rape of a sixteen year old. The acquired information was absolutely repulsive. I couldn't believe I came across someone like this. I requested a copy of the police report and received it after certain items were blacked out. His version of the story was disturbing.

He denied the allegations, claiming I was the one who initiated the sexual encounter. I immediately regretted my decision to not press charges and felt extreme hatred toward this individual. I certainly hope he didn't believe his own lie. There's no consent when a date rape drug is involved.

I desperately wanted to leave the company. I notified my supervisor about the police report, as well as my findings. I told him Brad was subtly harassing me at work by repeatedly passing by the work area, despite my instruction to stop. He had no business going up to another floor where he didn't belong. My supervisor said since the incident didn't occur at work, there was nothing they could do. It was challenging to find motivation to go into work. I regretted making a poor choice to hang out with Brad out of pity. I never thought a coworker would be capable of something this evil. I made several good male friends from various jobs. None of them hit on me or treated me with disrespect. I prayed God would help get me out of this situation. I searched for employment elsewhere to no avail. I continued to see my counselor who supported me throughout this traumatic event.

I'd like to add something out of the ordinary which happened two years after this incident. I was out shopping at a store, looking for a few items. Typically, I don't pay a great deal of attention to people around me when I'm in a store. As I walked down the aisle, I heard two men talking and didn't think anything of it. All of a sudden, I felt a strong negative vibe. Being caught off guard, I looked up toward the men who were nearby and saw Brad. My heart sank, and I rushed to the register immediately to check out. I prayed he didn't recognize me and especially hoped he wouldn't follow me.

To be safe, I didn't go straight home. Thankfully, nothing happened following our crossing paths. A flood of anxiety stuck with me for a bit because I wasn't sure if he recognized me at the store. I'm not sure how to explain what happened in a rational way. It's strange how I sensed an evil presence as a negative vibe, before becoming aware of Brad's presence. I can't stress enough how important it is to follow your gut instinct.

I decided to look up his public records again to see if anything new came up. Unfortunately, it did. In 2017, he ended up going to court to have his last name changed. What reason would he have to change his last name, unrelated to marriage? In 2018, there was a case involving domestic abuse with a temporary restraining order.

When it seems like the justice system fails, I rest assured knowing the God of justice, Elohim Mishpat, is omniscient and omnipotent. No one escapes His righteous judgement, as each one of us will be held accountable for our deeds here on Earth.

> But because of your stubbornness and your unrepentant heart, you are storing up wrath against yourself for the day of God's wrath, when his righteous judgment will be revealed. God 'will repay each person according to what they have done.' To those who by persistence in doing good seek glory,

honor and immortality, he will give eternal life. But for those who are self seeking and who reject the truth and follow evil, there will be wrath and anger. There will be trouble and distress for every human being who does evil. (Rom. 2:5–9 NIV)

We will all stand before God's judgment seat. It is written: 'As surely as I live,' says the Lord, 'every knee will bow before me; every tongue will acknowledge God.' So then, each of us will give an account of ourselves to God. (Rom. 14:10–12 NIV)

The Lord reigns forever; he has established his throne for judgment. He rules the world in righteousness and judges the peoples with equity. The Lord is a refuge for the oppressed, a stronghold in times of trouble. Those who know your name trust in you, for you, Lord, have never forsaken those who seek you. (Psa. 9:7–10 NIV)

Do not repay anyone evil for evil. Be careful to do what is right in the eyes of everyone. If it is possible, as far as it depends on you, live at peace with everyone. Do not take revenge, my dear friends, but leave room for God's wrath, for it is written: 'It is mine to avenge; I will repay,' says the Lord. Do not be overcome by evil, but overcome evil with good. (Rom. 12:17–19, 21 NIV)

8

OBEDIENCE TO GOD AND PLACING HIM FIRST IS KEY

I'll now redirect the story to talk about another lesson in the midst of this challenging situation. Keep in mind this account is written from my point of view. There are always two sides to every story.

Kyle was an online friend who initially sent me a message through a Christian dating site four years prior, somewhere around 2012. When we first talked, he was about twenty three years old, and I was about twenty nine. I questioned our age difference of six years, but he appeared to be a nice person. I held the opinion younger men don't know what they want. They didn't take things seriously, weren't mature, and weren't responsible. I felt I didn't have much in common with them. For some reason, they often pursued me. I'm mature for my age, and in my experience, dating younger men always proved to be a headache.

Stereotypes aside, Kyle and I stayed in touch off and on throughout those four years. We lived four hours apart, so hanging out was out of the question. There was a handful of times we planned to meet face to face, but something always came up. I figured he chickened out and let it go at that.

The more we got to know each other, the more I liked him. I felt he was the type of person I was looking for. When we talked on the phone, I enjoyed hearing his voice and the way he talked. There was a sense of innocence to him. He had a funny sense of humor, was old fashioned, hardworking, and had a child of his own. It seemed he possessed the same morals and values I had.

In one of our conversations, he mentioned he wanted a Christian woman and wished he could find someone like me, which I thought was cute. We talked about various topics in the time we knew each other. There were times I'd ask him for advice from a male's perspective. He talked to me more than usual during the winter of 2015, and I wondered why. This was the time period where I transitioned from the nursing home job to the electrical assembly job.

In January 2016, I invited him to attend my birthday celebration. He accepted the invitation in order to finally meet me. Despite letting me down in the past, I thought he was going to make it this time. He was sure he could attend, up until the day before the party. He couldn't find a sitter for his son.

That was the last straw. I decided to give up on ever meeting him. After Kyle's rejection, my interactions with him decreased, and I kept our conversations brief. He must have eventually picked up on that. Out of the blue, he told me we have to meet, and he was going to make it work no matter what. I didn't believe him but went along with it. We planned to meet half way in Madison, and while I waited for him to chicken out again, he didn't. I was hesitant and was getting ready to leave, waiting for a last minute cancellation, but to my surprise, it didn't happen.

We met up at a restaurant in the small town where I used to live and hit it off pretty well. At this point we knew a lot about each other, being friends for four years. I felt comfortable around him. I enjoyed his personality and believed he was everything I wanted in a man. His presence made me happy. I guess you could say it was a "butterflies in the stomach" kind of feeling.

As we walked around downtown Madison sightseeing, he asked to hold my hand. I wasn't used to that type of courtesy. No one ever asked permission to hold my hand. Following the walk downtown, we drove back toward the restaurant, which was located right on the lake. At this point, the sun had set. There were a few benches nearby, overlooking the lake, and we decided to sit there to talk.

Out of nowhere, it started to rain. Since we didn't want to end the conversation, we drove to the local bowling alley. It was getting late, and Kyle didn't think it'd be a good idea to make the two hour drive home. He decided to crash at the hotel. I chose to stay with him, so he wouldn't be alone. I wondered if I made the right decision. Sleeping in the same bed could've risked the temptation to become intimate. I brushed off the thought, seeing how he appeared to be a respectable person, and I had no intentions of becoming intimate.

My desire to wait until marriage remained, even though I failed to stay committed to that pledge many times before. Whenever I failed in the past, I told myself "This is it! I won't do it again and I mean it this time. I'll be strong and not give in!" The emotional pain of becoming intimate with men who were no good for me, nor had the desire for marriage was becoming increasingly devastating to me. My heart felt like it couldn't take any more rejection and pain. The greatest pain was the heartache of separating myself from any man who I became intimate with and developed feelings for.

In the past, I talked with Kyle about my desire to wait until marriage to become intimate. I vented about my experiences with men who took advantage and how my heart was broken. Unfortunately, he must have not remembered. I won't go into detail but when I asked him later what happened, he said he "couldn't contain himself." I know I also have to accept responsibility because I failed to remind him of my desire to wait. I had plenty of opportunity to discuss the importance of this issue throughout our entire date, yet I remained silent. I'd later regret that decision.

It was clear we liked each other. The hard part was trying to figure out how to make this work. We visited each other on weekends that worked with our schedules. It wasn't long before he asked me to be his girlfriend. I said yes without any hesitation. I made my intentions clear to Kyle regarding marriage. I had no desire to be in a short term relationship and was seeking a husband. I mentioned this in a previous discussion but wanted to bring it up again in case he forgot. Kyle affirmed he was ready to settle down, start a family life, and get married.

I thought, *This is finally it! God has given me the husband I've been waiting years for*! As we continued the long distance relationship, he told me how he felt. He loved how we shared the same morals and values. He told me I was kind, caring, and attractive. Before I knew it, Kyle blurted out the "I love you" on the phone. He wanted to wait until he saw me face to face but couldn't hold off any longer. I never thought any man truly saw those qualities in me.

Kyle spoke kindly to me and treated me like no one else had. I fell for his old fashioned manners and the courtesy of asking to hold my hand or to give me a kiss. He opened doors for me and used silly phrases I thought were adorable. There were absolutely no red flags. When I thought about what I looked for in a man, he possessed *all* of the qualities. I truly thought it was impossible to find. People have told me in the past I was "too picky" because my list of qualifications was extensive. And the older I got, the longer the list became!

It felt like things were getting serious between us. Looking at it from an outside perspective, you'd think it would be unwise to move this fast in such a short period of time. While we met online four years before, it was only after a few short months after meeting face to face that we got to this point. We were in love and talking about marriage.

Since I felt this was it, I met my future husband, I knew eventually one of us would've to relocate. I took many things into consideration. At the time, I didn't have much holding me down. I lived with my parents and had no intention staying at my job. I also had full custody of Damon. Kyle had a lot of responsibilities back home. In addition to working full time, he tended to some animals that were kept on the family farm, which he was expected to take over in the near future. He also had biweekly custody of his son. It was clear I'd have to be the one to make a sacrifice.

Deep down, I knew it wasn't wise to move in with a partner without being married, but given the circumstances, I ignored my internal nagging voice. I assumed since Kyle was my future husband, it didn't matter. Believe me when I say, don't ignore your internal nagging voice. We came to the decision I was going to move as soon as I found a job. It was an exciting time. Kyle often told me I was "stuck with him for good," and he was happy to settle down with me. He regularly told me how much he loved me. We met each other's family and got along wonderfully. The lifestyle he lived was something I always dreamed of but never thought would happen for me.

Searching for social service jobs in the area proved unsuccessful. I became impatient and decided to try manufacturing in the meantime. Once I got acquainted with the area, it'd be easier to locate a job where I could utilize my degree. I eventually got hired as an electrical assembler in June 2016. Damon spent the summer break with my parents, which made things easier. I wouldn't be able to afford childcare with a decreased income.

When I moved, I only brought up what I needed for the month until Kyle's roommate moved out. I arrived shortly before starting my new job and a few days before Kyle had to leave for his annual two week training for the National Guard. While he was in training, I stayed with his grandmother, Dorothy. The scenery in this small northwestern Wisconsin town magnificently portrayed God's handiwork. It seemed the sun always shone, the skies and vegetation were unpolluted, and the peace of nature was beautifully evident. I was accustomed to polluted city life, where even the "country" appeared contaminated. My heart felt like it belonged here.

Kyle's two week leave turned out to be quite difficult, which we didn't see coming. My insecurities began to surface. I noticed this and wondered why I was insecure. He and I were on different levels when it came to standpoints on socialization, communication, and I suppose the use of social media and technology. I tend to be simpler and prefer to communicate in old fashioned ways. I enjoy face to face interactions and being in other people's presence, without the distraction of a cell phone.

It's fairly difficult to be present when you have people contending for attention on your phone. I admit there are times when I'm distracted by texting, but it's not often. I enjoy living in the moment, appreciating the company of others, as well as my surroundings.

At that time in my life, I refused to have a smart phone because when I looked at the world around me, I observed people glued to those little devices. In my opinion, having a phone addiction is a wasted life. It portrays disrespect and self centeredness to those who are in their midst attempting to have conversation. I saw Kyle had those moments, which brought up my hidden insecurities.

I reflected back on past observations and experiences relating to people who are secretive about their phones. I've witnessed situations where someone would become angry if you jokingly took or even touched their phone, which reveals they had something to hide. You often hear about people using social media apps to secretly cheat on spouses. I've known people who were affected by them. Thankfully, God has continued to work on my self esteem as time goes on. I'll give an illustration of a negative experience I had involving a younger boyfriend. This took place somewhere around 2010.

I observed him often looking at other women when we were together, which led me to feel highly insecure about myself. It appeared he didn't want to be in a serious relationship with me, so I wondered what his intentions were. Did he just want to have fun? I tested him by creating a fake profile on the site where he initially messaged me, which is how we got to know one another. To give you the gist of what happened, he told the "fake" person he was in a relationship, but since he thought she was pretty, he decided to make plans to have intercourse. When I confronted him about it, he called me, crying and apologizing. I felt no sympathy toward him and immediately ended the relationship. I was completely heartbroken and suffered another emotional scar caused by rejection.

Looking back now, I realize my tendency to give my entire heart to whoever it is I developed a relationship with. I'd exhaust myself putting a great deal of effort in to make things work, but the work produced no fruit. I ended up bearing the burden alone while the man I was trying to please had ill intentions all along.

Always remember, it takes two to make a relationship work. If you're the only one trying to resolve conflict, you'll carry the burden alone. Working together toward conflict resolution is critical for a successful relationship. I'm no expert, but this should be common sense.

Giving my whole heart to a man is where I have erred because my whole heart should be dedicated to the Lord. I don't understand why I feel strong connections with people, whether it's through friendships, professional acquaintances, or relationships. I believe it may be related to the Holy Spirit dwelling within. "Do you not know that your bodies are temples of the Holy Spirit, who is in you, whom you have received from God? You are not your own" (1 Cor. 6:19 NIV).

Back to where I left off in the story involving Kyle: he went on his phone quite a bit. Even after getting into a relationship with me, I noticed he continued to "like" other women's racy pictures on social media. Additionally, he befriended a woman whose profile was exceptionally distasteful. She posted half naked pictures, displaying her phone number. I wondered how in the world he met this woman. When he noticed I became a bit withdrawn following these observations, I explained why. I expressed how it made me uncomfortable seeing various pages he liked in his profile that objectified women. I have strong feelings against anything that portrays women in a distasteful way—especially pornography. The key point is that it's sinful.

You can tell a lot about a person through their social media profiles. You see where their interests lie, the type of friends they associate with, and so forth. Sometimes people are not careful how they portray themselves. Kyle ended up unfriending the questionable woman he recently added and took the offensive pages off his profile, which I appreciated. He said he didn't know who the woman was, he just accepted her request because they had a mutual friend.

Aside from our social differences, we recognized other conflicting points of view. Kyle didn't seem to understand where

I came from, in regard to having a biblical worldview. He didn't think certain behaviors were wrong because he didn't understand sin. This discovery threw me off. I assumed he knew what sin was. I had to explain the biblical point of view to someone who claimed to be a Christian.

Kyle began to second guess our relationship shortly before it was time for him to return home from training. One day he was unsure if it was going to work out between us. Another day he wanted to make it work. His doubts caused me to feel anxious, depressed, and nauseous. I no longer felt secure in our relationship, as he easily wanted to give up.

This emotional roller coaster led me to break down and cry. I wondered why God placed me here if I was going to be leaving just a few weeks later. I made a great sacrifice moving four hours away for the man I thought was destined to be my husband. I believe my faith was being put to the test.

I came across a Christian radio station and was drawn to a program that came on when I left for work each morning. It reminded me of sermons from my home church. The pastor preached over books of the Bible chapter by chapter. At the time, he went through the book of Samuel. I craved hearing the message because I hadn't found a church since the move. I didn't know anyone in the area to tell me about any local Bible teaching churches. I was glad I came across this radio program. Many of the messages were beneficial as they sometimes related to problems I experienced and taught how to deal with them.

One day the pastor's message was on the topic of waiting in relation to God's will. He briefly used Abraham and Isaac as an example of God's timing, taken from Genesis 22. He explained if something is truly God's will, He'll provide an answer to you at the exact moment you need it. Just as Abraham was about to plunge the knife down to sacrifice his son Isaac, the angel of the Lord called to him at just the right time.

That message stood out to me, and I didn't understand why. I questioned my future with Kyle. I prayed for the Lord's will to be done, and if God wanted me to stay, I'd stay. If He wanted me to go back home, I'd go. I didn't want to do anything outside of God's plans because I know Abba Father knows best. After hearing the sermon, I felt God was going to give me an answer at the last second, as a way to test my faith. All I could do was wait.

What ended up happening caught me off guard and put me through another emotional roller coaster. I felt in my heart Kyle was ready to give up. I left it up to him to decide what he wanted and he remained set that it would be best for me to go back home. His mother, Anna, acted as a mediator via telephone, between the two of us. This took place in Dorothy's driveway where I was loading my car. Anna said he told her he loved me and didn't want me to leave, but he didn't know what to do. He didn't tell me this during our interactions, and I couldn't understand why. I told Anna what Kyle told me, "Maybe it's best if I go back home where all my support is." He did not once tell me to stay.

I told them both, since Kyle thought it was best I go back home, that I was going to pack and leave, even though I desperately wanted to stay and make it work. I had no desire to give up in our relationship, but knew I couldn't force him to be with me if he didn't want to. Deep down, I sensed God was going to respond at the last second. It appeared Kyle wasn't going to budge. I hadn't told anyone back home about what was going on because in my heart, I felt I was meant to stay, despite the circumstances. Something inside told me to not say a word to anyone.

My car was finally loaded with whatever belongings I could fit into it. I then sent a text to Kyle telling him I was about to go. I planned on making the phone call to my family once I was on the road home. Anna tried to talk me out of it. I felt I was being stalled, but again, I wasn't sure. I didn't want to appear rude, so I let her continue talking, even though I felt like I shouldn't delay the inevitable.

To my surprise, Kyle called me. He said, "Don't go; I want you to stay." He explained he wanted to call earlier but was commanded to work on something. When he returned to his phone, he saw my message. I suddenly remembered the radio message. I cried in relief, seeing he didn't want to give up. A few days later, he returned home from training.

9

TRUST IN THE LORD WHEN THINGS DON'T GO AS EXPECTED

Following our near breakup, I made sure to communicate openly, even about tough things that were difficult for me to talk about. I'm a strong believer in communication, especially in a relationship. Kyle told me he felt the same, but over time, I realized that wasn't necessarily true. Whenever a minor conflict arose, he distanced himself and avoided the topic. He was "too tired to think about it," and expressed other excuses. There were times where he would eventually think about it and allow a conversation to take place. During those talks, we apologized and recognized where we needed change. Change is always necessary to help people grow.

The love I had for Kyle was strong, so I was willing to do whatever it took to make our relationship work. I desired to put effort into changing things I knew I needed to work on. I also wanted to help him make the changes he needed, in order to help us grow together. It was evident how much I loved him. Love isn't only a word; it's an action. I expressed forgiveness, patience, kindness, and empathy. I did whatever I could at home to make his life easier by cooking, cleaning, running errands, and offering to help with tasks.

At this point in my life, I was ready to be a wife. I was committed to work on a successful marriage in the way it should be done. As I explained previously, my former church taught on the biblical instruction for marriage and led by example. Additionally, I read Christian based articles about relationships to prepare for success. God knows I desired marriage more than anything.

Throughout the increasing times of uncertainty in my relationship with Kyle, I turned to God for help. It seemed Kyle wasn't fulfilling his word on putting effort into change, and he reverted to his old habits of running from conflict. Once again, I was led to go into nature to meet with the Lord and pray. I received much comfort knowing He's in control of all things. I continued to seek Him in the most beautiful, isolated place I could find. It's always there where I feel His presence and listen to Him speak in that still, small voice. I focus on His presence in the wind, the warm sun, and the running waters, and hear Him in the stillness. There are never distractions.

When I set time aside to meet with the Almighty, the peace I feel is unexplainable. Even in the most chaotic situations, He can give peace to the most troubled soul. I was uncertain if Kyle had any intention to marry me because he stopped talking about it. He didn't tell me he loved me as much as he did before. He wouldn't express his feelings to me about anything. The person I knew seemed to have changed into someone else.

At this point in time, I hadn't realized I gave my whole heart to another person, rather than my Heavenly Father—to whom it's due. Unfortunately, my heart was divided. I truly believed Kyle was the one God had for me as a husband, but his tendency to give up easily and run from conflict were indicators of alarm. I became fearful and anxious. My health was rapidly declining due to the stress I felt. It was clearly obvious because coworkers began to look at me in a concerning manner. There were two specific circumstances I can recall when I went out to pray about my uncertainty.

These two circumstances involve a miraculous event. Almost immediately after I prayed on the nature trail, I felt such a wonderful peace. It was even visibly evident. My look of "death" disappeared, my energy was restored, and I started to smile and laugh again. This peace stayed with me for a little while, and Kyle wondered what happened. He saw it and couldn't believe it. He thought I may have even been faking it. I couldn't explain how it happened because it was, in fact, a miracle. I believe this was meant to serve as an example to Kyle of what God can truly do for His children.

I knew God was going to work this out, and I knew I moved out there for a purpose. I pondered why the Lord would have me move far from home if Kyle and I weren't meant to be. I prayed for His will to be done, and it all fell into place. I kept in mind the moment I waited on God to give me the answer on whether or not I should stay and the confirmation I received. My heart remained certain that we were meant to be together.

Sadly, my inner peace faded when I realized how much work and effort I was putting into the relationship. It wasn't equally exchanged. I exhausted myself trying to make it work. I paid attention to several excuses he made when it came to growing together. He was still always "too tired or too busy." There were several instances where it became evident Kyle and I were at different levels spiritually. He wouldn't read any Christian articles I sent his way. He declined counsel offered by the elders of my former church. He refused to locate a Bible teaching church with me, insisting the one he grew up in was good enough.

His grandmother, Dorothy, was a regular attendee, while Kyle seldom went. In the few services we attended together, I discovered they didn't teach God's Word. The sermons didn't seem to address the sin problem, pointing to our need for a Savior. After observing Kyle's behavior, and hearing Dorothy regularly gossip about others, I came to the conclusion that it was all superficial. They didn't have the love of Christ in them. The Holy Spirit didn't dwell in their hearts; otherwise they'd be compelled to love others with a humble heart. This was disappointing.

Aside from our spiritual differences, Kyle wasn't interested in spending quality time with me in order to get to know each other better. He got upset when I verbalized my desire to find a Bible teaching church in the area to make new friends. I wish I could've seen it in the beginning, but his behaviors were becoming increasingly concerning. It felt like he was purposely trying to isolate me. He stopped introducing me to his friends, and I saw less and less of his family.

Since I didn't have friends of my own in the area, I vented to a trusted coworker, Brenda, about what I was going through. Brenda told me a story about someone she knew who went through a similar experience. This woman was in a relationship with a man who treated her poorly. He'd tell her to leave and when she was ready to leave, he begged her to stay. Brenda said this went on for years, and they eventually got married, but her friend divorced the man because he didn't change. Her husband was indecisive, and she couldn't handle it anymore.

The more I thought about her story, the more I realized the same thing was happening to me. Kyle wasn't changing and remained inconsistent. I didn't know what to do, so I continued to pray. I tried my best to be civil in the midst of our struggles. I desperately wanted to grow into a better person by handling conflict in healthier ways. What I wanted most was for us to communicate openly and effectively. I knew what worked best for me and tried to explain it to Kyle, so he could approach potential arguments with careful consideration.

For example, if something bothered me, I became quiet and distant. He'd ask what was wrong and wanted me to tell him right away. I preferred to remain quiet for the time being, in order to think of an appropriate way to express my thoughts. However, his impatience led me to open up at a time I wasn't ready, which caused intense anxiety and led to unnecessary arguments. Kyle swore he wouldn't get upset the next time I got quiet about a topic that bothered me. Unfortunately, his inconsistency proved otherwise. What ended up happening triggered an unexpected series of events. Here's what happened.

A conversation came up where we had an opportunity to discuss an issue in a civilized manner. It was a chance to put conflict resolution into practice. It started off okay. This particular discussion involved his child's mother, Shelly. As time went on, Shelly's unusual behaviors made me feel progressively uncomfortable, and I was embarrassed by her immaturity. My embarrassment increased when other people inquired about her actions, questioning why she sought a lot of attention. This was done both in person and through social media. I was curious as well, which led to the discussion at hand.

During the conversation, Kyle became angry and defensive. He talked about past arguments to "prove his points." I was brought to tears defending myself against his verbal attacks. He insisted I was in the wrong, I gave up arguing and the dispute ended. Later, I was convicted to apologize and asked for Kyle's forgiveness. Resolving conflicts are critical, and apologies are always a step in the right direction. Kyle remained agitated and felt he was justified in his anger. He didn't admit to doing any wrong, and when I attempted to talk about the benefits of forgiveness, he refused to forgive me. He wanted to stay angry.

That's when it hit me like a ton of bricks. Kyle wasn't a genuine Christian. He didn't understand forgiveness and surely didn't demonstrate it. My soft heart went from feeling utter sadness to hardened anger. I angrily shouted at him for deceiving me into believing he was Christian. The one thing I wanted in a husband. My intense anger surprised me.

It was as if my heart shriveled up and turned black as night. Days went by where I didn't say much of anything to Kyle. It seemed my worst nightmare was coming true.

Several questions raced through my mind— "Am I going to have to leave? Were his words about spending his life with me just a lie? I sacrificially moved my entire life hours from home to be with him, and this is how he repays me? He's going to just throw my love away like it's nothing?"

He attempted to make casual conversation following my angry outburst. I remained mostly silent, and my face was expressionless. Kyle was ignoring the problem. His inappropriate response did nothing to appease my frustration. It only confirmed what must take place.

On August 15, 2016, I submitted applications online for jobs back home. Kyle arrived home later than usual and asked when I was going to leave. I told him I was looking for work but didn't plan on being around long. I had paid my half of the rent for the month, so I knew I had some time to make arrangements. I wanted to secure employment before moving to ensure my bills were paid on time.

He continued to pressure me about moving and asked if I wanted him to pick up boxes to pack my belongings. I told him I didn't need his help because when we argued about me leaving the last time, he refused to take part in any of it.

Kyle once again provoked me to anger as he attempted to take control over this situation. He insulted my intelligence and his lack of empathy prompted feelings of resentment. I could no longer stand to be in his presence.

I told him I was going to sleep in my car and gathered a few items. I loudly expressed harsh and hateful words toward Kyle as he quietly sat there. It didn't affect me in the moment because I was overtaken by rage. Once I grabbed what I needed, I stormed out to my car and drove somewhere low key. I set my alarm for work and slept uncomfortably in the car. It wasn't anything I couldn't handle. Thankfully, it was summertime.

When the alarm went off, I decided to go home to take a shower first. I knew Kyle would've already left for work. When I arrived home, the deadbolts and doorknobs were locked on both doors. We never locked the doorknobs and I was only given a key to the deadbolt. I couldn't believe it.

I told him in a text message he couldn't lock me out of my own home because I had to get ready for work. He refused to negotiate. I told him I didn't want to have to get hold of the police but would do so if he didn't let me in. He said, "The police or the landlord can get hold of me." I had no choice but to contact the police department and explain what happened.

LIFE LESSON

After I got off the phone, the officer told Kyle to meet us at the apartment. Being a small town, I believed the officer might present a bias if he and Kyle knew each other. When they arrived, I provided my side of the story. I asked if I could press charges and was told I couldn't. My mind was completely overwhelmed, and I felt sick to my stomach. The officer questioned our living arrangement because he didn't know I lived there. I told him I submitted paperwork to the landlord in order to add my name to the lease. I've been paying my share of the rent and utilities since I moved in a few short months ago. I insisted Kyle had no right to lock me out of my own home, where all my belongings were located.

I couldn't live like this anymore. Kyle was causing massive emotional turmoil, and it needed to stop. I decided enough was enough. I couldn't delay the inevitable any longer. I told the policeman I wanted to contact my employer and start packing my things, so I could be out as soon as possible. After I was let in, the officer spoke to Kyle separately. He then went back to work.

My first task was to call my supervisor. I told him I had to move back to Kenosha. He felt bad about the situation and expressed understanding. I also called my family to tell them what was going on. My next task was to start packing what wasn't already boxed up. Thankfully, I had extra boxes stashed in the basement to use from the last time Kyle threatened our relationship. Once I ran out, I went to a nearby store to grab more.

The burst of energy I received was miraculous. The severe stress I endured led to a reduced appetite. I wasn't eating much of anything—a result of being "lovesick." In the two short months I lived with Kyle, I lost approximately ten pounds from stress. My clothes became loose fitting, my eyes were baggy, and I looked like death.

I searched online to rent a truck big enough to make one trip as soon as possible. By God's grace, I found one half an hour away, available for pick up the same day. There was only one person I could turn to for help—Sandy who took me to pick up the rental that evening and offered her sons to help load the heavier furniture. I told her I was appreciative of her support because I couldn't do it all alone. The moment we got the last piece of heavy furniture in, is when it started to downpour. That was an indication to stop.

Anna convinced Kyle to stay the night with family, so we didn't have to spend the evening together. He stopped by after work to pick up a few overnight items. When he told me this, I continued to pack silently, with my head down. It was the last night I'd sleep in this beautiful, small country town that I had come to love. God surely intervened to make this all work together. I don't know how it was possible to get it all taken care of in one day, especially given the condition I was in. It was yet another example of how God shows His strength and gives strength to His children.

> I know that you can do all things; no purpose of Yours can be thwarted. (Job 42:2 NIV)

> I can do all things through Him (Christ) who gives me strength. (Phil. 4:13 NIV)

Before my family arrived the next afternoon, I managed to load the remaining totes and boxes into the truck, with the exception of a few items. My energy was sustained by drinking a few protein shakes over the course of those two days. I still hadn't eaten solid foods due to my loss of appetite. I left the apartment spotless and rearranged it exactly how it was before I moved in. Despite feeling hatred toward Kyle, I still felt the need to show kindness. I left behind several items and toys for his child that Damon no longer wanted or needed. Finally, I double checked to make sure I didn't leave anything behind. I didn't want to come back. I then placed his key in the mailbox and told him it was all done. He was working at the time.

It was unreal. I truly believed in my heart Kyle was the one, otherwise I wouldn't have made such a tremendous sacrifice. I couldn't believe what was happening. I knew I wasn't stable enough to drive due to the emotional state I was in. There were moments I broke down and cried while driving on the interstate, sobbing in the most pitiful manner. The tears wouldn't stop coming. How was I going to tell everyone things didn't work out between me and Kyle?

This was my third time moving in six months. Though I had become accustomed to moving frequently, it gets quite tiring and overwhelmingly stressful. A lot of tasks are involved when it comes to moving. I had to complete another change of address form with the post office. I had to update my address with the various companies who mail out my billing statements. I had to temporarily deactivate the new modem I purchased for my laptop because there was no use for it back home. I couldn't afford any unnecessary bills without a job. I had to figure out where to store my belongings again. I had to register Damon back to his old school, after going through the headache of registering him for the one up north.

I had to start all over—again.

10

EARTH HAS NO SORROW THAT HEAVEN CANNOT HEAL (THOMAS MOORE) [2]

Once I settled into my parents' home in Kenosha, I continued to search for employment. Thankfully, I had enough money saved to continue paying my bills. Finances were the least of my worries for the moment.

I had difficulty adjusting to the circumstances and wanted to escape what felt like a negative environment. My deteriorated state required some sort of action. I decided to do what I always did when I felt alone and hopeless. I went out into nature to meet with the Lord in desperation. I wasn't sure what to expect because I felt abandoned by God, following the unexpected outcome of my recent relationship.

I chose to alternate going to two individual parks on a daily basis, primarily because their trails were more isolated. I alternated for the change of scenery, as well as physically and spiritually feeling the Lord's presence within each park. There were specific places on these trails where I was guided to sit on either a log or a rock, located right by the water.

On August 29, 2016 I started to journal, as I felt led to write. I was unsure why at the time, but figured it'd help release my thoughts and feelings, as I had done sparingly in the past. Not long after I began to write in my journal, I recognized its potential purpose. Journaling helped me reflect on revelations God revealed to me. Since my memory has fragmented throughout my adult years, writing in a journal proved helpful to remember God's presence and peace during troubled times. Early entries typically begin by venting my frustrations to God, asking why I have to suffer so much. Then, my later entries include praises of how God intervened and healed me through the storm.

Journaling revealed the fact my suffering wasn't permanent, and God's blessings were much greater in the aftermath. It resulted in a life lesson learned, as well as a greater dependence on the Lord Almighty to handle my concerns. I often pondered what might have happened if things continued in my own will versus the Lord's will.

As I looked through the journal entries in the midst of my despair, I saw God's work in the healing process. I noticed a fluctuation of emotions as they ranged from anger, hope, sadness, peace, doubt, joy, and trust. It exposed the instability of my mind, which is quite honestly embarrassing. My first entry on August 29, 2016 confirms God's work immediately. I described how I felt the Lord's presence and peace whenever I went out to meet with Him, and the chaos of my mind returned once I left our meeting place. When I wrote this particular entry, I went to the park to pray about my confusion over what happened.

At the time, I was unsure if the Lord was speaking to me or if I was deceiving myself. The elder of my church once told us in a sermon there are three voices we hear as believers: our own voice, the voice of the Holy Spirit, and the voice of our enemy, Satan. Throughout this time, I was unsure whose voice I heard but decided to write it all down anyway.

For the remainder of this chapter, I'll include some condensed journal entries to show where I was psychologically during this season. You'll be exposed to the madness, which flooded my heart and soul during this frustrating time. As previously mentioned, my emotions ranged across the board.

Much of the earlier entries focus on confusion regarding Kyle. By the end, you'll notice I was freed from the chains of depression and received healing by letting go of what wasn't meant to be. These journal entries span over a period of around eight months. I conclude this chapter with an unexpected revelation I received about three years later.

You'll notice brief references about things that were going on at the time, which makes it appear I'm jumping ahead of the story. I began the next chapter where I left off in the narrative, so those details will be covered as I continue telling my story.

For your reference, I quoted what I heard the Lord speak to me. Or to explain it in a way that's easier to understand—it was the still, small voice I heard from inside. You'll notice a few contradictions involving who is meant to be my true husband. What I think may be the case, is I was meant to forgive Kyle and his family, pray for their salvation, and await my true husband.

Due to the length of the journal entries, I broke them up into categories highlighting the various, fluctuating stages of the healing process: chaos, hope, comfort in letting go, acceptance, and continued growth through the pain, trust, patience, and peace.

CHAOS

8/29/16

Though I wish I could've written this earlier, some days after my experience, I couldn't find my journal notebook to write it down. Here I am improvising. When I went to the park to pray and sit with the Lord—anxious, sad, depressed and stressed—I heard Him speak to me. I wasn't sure if it was my own thoughts deceiving me, hoping Kyle would come back, as I was certain and sure he was the one for me. What happened turned out to be the opposite. Since coming home, I've been going out daily to my peaceful place on the trails with the Lord, praying and asking for answers. It's there I feel His presence and peace and am at rest. Once I leave, the chaos in my mind sets in all over again. I prayed for God to give me a sign that it's Him I hear and not me deceiving myself. I heard Him tell me He'll give me a sign. The next day, I went to our bridge at the other park and stopped by the water, the other place I meet with Him. I looked down at the wooden rail and saw a cross carved out. That was my sign, and I knew it instantly. I again felt peace and His presence and His words comforted me. He tells me to 'let it go and trust Him.' Once I let it go, He can do His work in Kyle.

Before this experience in making daily trips to meet with the Lord in my two locations, I went to write a letter to Kyle after receiving confirmation from my pastor and elder that it'd be a good idea to write a handwritten letter to apologize for my harsh words. Pastor's sermon in James 3:1–12 about taming the tongue convicted me. I went to my place of peace at the park, feeling led to bring my Bible along and write. I don't know how the words came to me so clearly, as well as the Scripture references, but it happened. I felt the Holy Spirit working, because in that time my mind and emotions were still out of whack and in shock of the whole situation (this letter was written less than one week after my return home). It was an unhealthy situation, and I don't think the Lord wanted me to continue in it. He allowed me the resources and assistance to move back quickly.

It was extremely painful, and even now I'm still in the process of healing from yet another broken heart. There is always hope, even when I don't see it. I see things as they are now, but God sees it all and has greater things in store for me. As I write this on my bridge over the water, I feel Him in the wind again. He said, the timing was bad on our part; I need to now wait for Him to work in Kyle's heart. While I fear it may take many years, as Kyle is a person of excuses and procrastination, I know God can work miracles. I'll wait patiently on God and not put my trust in Kyle. Though he cut my heart deeply, I don't know the whole picture. God is a God of miracles—remember this.

Remember who I once was. I was unemployed, brokenhearted, stressed, and confused, but God saw me through it.

He (God) asked me what I wanted most. This was brought up Sunday in Cecil's message about how Solomon was asked this question by God and he asked for wisdom. I had no idea what to ask for that I wanted most. Different ideas kept running through my mind and it was hard to choose. He said He'll give me a hint, it was something that kept repeating in my mind. Peace. Continuous peace. My world is chaos right now, and peace would most definitely alleviate the chaos in my mind, heart, and soul.

The enemy has definitely played with my mind and health for months now. He cannot harm me any longer as long as I continue to fix my eyes on Jesus. Put my trust in Him. Rely on His words versus my own or Satan's. Maybe the reason I went through all the suffering from June until now was to lead me to a place closer with God. To meet with Him. To place Him first again rather than Kyle or myself. It is another life lesson.

The peace this place brings me is unreal. I see an otter, a heron, a turtle, and fish. The crickets are singing, the water is running, the breeze is cool, and the sun is warm. God is here. No distractions. My phone never goes off while I'm here, though it rarely does anyway. He wants me to write, though I never understand why, knowing my thoughts don't make sense, and I don't feel that I'm a good writer. I think it's to help me remember how I overcome many trials with Him near my side. My memory is quite bad so this makes sense.

The next time I suffer, I'll pull out my writings to remember where I came from. God really does love me. I also felt the love of my church family coming back. They treat us kindly and welcoming as always. That is the love of God. *True* love in action. I sent a picture of my daily devotional page to Kyle via email, and he responded the next day. I responded by saying I hope he received my letter. He confirmed saying it was a good read. Unfortunately, he's been "too busy" to search the Bible for answers (as I encouraged him to do in the letter). But there is hope. God confirmed that he needs a lot of work and that it'll take time. I need to let it go and trust God.

8/30/16

I met with my mentor today and talked some more. The tears and emotions are still here with me I noticed. But the peace I feel is more prevalent. I know it'll work out. My church family is praying for my two job interviews today. My mentor shared an article with me that was spot on to my situation. What stood out most, besides the recurring theme of trust I've been receiving in various forms, is while I believe God *can* move in my circumstances, I don't yet have enough faith to say God *will*. Trust is the key word He's presently repeating to me.

I'm at the park writing and will pray for a job. I'm nervous, but I know God is with me in this and *will* provide a good job for me. I just recalled the time up north where I was down and felt alone, upset, and uncertain about my future, particularly with Kyle. I went on the trail up there and prayed desperately for peace. I prayed it also at work another time and received it almost instantly. I felt better, not sick, and it was visibly evident.

Kyle noticed it and said I looked good and wondered what happened. He wasn't sure if I was faking it. I told him how and why it happened. I couldn't explain it how it was miraculous. I believe it was God showing him an example of faith and His work. Kyle couldn't understand how I could've received peace in that situation, as well as seeing me smiling again, being loving, patient, reassuring, and confident that God would work it out. Now things happened to where we are no longer together, but I'm sure God has a purpose for it.

8/31/16

Today I felt a little bit of sadness and hopelessness. I'm not sure where those feelings came from since these last few days were more peaceful as I have been sitting here by Lake Michigan where it's windy, the waves are crashing on the rocks and the sun is setting. I've cried but held in tears while I'm with Damon. I have to be strong in front of him as hard as that is. My heavenly Father asked why I let the peace escape me. I don't know why. I'm supposed to trust Him and peace remains with that. I just don't feel Kyle will put forth the effort to change or care to.

I doubt Kyle's efforts, but God tells me not to put my trust in man but in Him alone. Why can't I do that consistently? I am hopeless. I want a job. I also want Kyle but don't at the same time. Is it me or God saying Kyle will be how he once was; he just buried it deep inside? Oh, how I need patience, faith and trust. My hope feels like it left. The enemy must have taken over my mind.

God is telling me to look at the waters, the land and the sky. He keeps it all in balance and is in control of it all—of the whole universe. How could He not work out my little situation? I feel like the crashing waves are pulling me under, suffering. Does it end? It's always one thing to the next, but I suppose that's the result of my sins. My just punishment for disobedience when I should know better. Why do I keep on sinning? Does suffering indeed make me stronger? God says it does. I just want peace, stability, love, a place to call home, safety, and consistency. Will I ever have it in this life? This instant I feel pain, heartache, isolation, loneliness, sadness, and hopelessness. Please go away. I want the joy of Jesus.

HOPE

9/1/16

God hears. He knows. I received a call about the service coordinator position for the homeless. I have an interview next week with them. My hope is being restored, as I prayed it would. I realized the three places that called me for interviews—whether on the phone or in person were jobs I dreamed of. It helps me to remember God knows the desires of my heart and is working in my life. I don't know what will come of these, but I trust God will lead me to the right one. There really is hope. One thing at a time.

If I get a job soon, then I can move out and it'll be me, Damon, and Misty (our cat) again like it once was. God wants that, too. He knows it's hard living with the family. I'm now reminded of something my elder once said in a sermon: the one thing we want most in life is the thing we have to wait the longest for. At that time, my thought was a husband. This was before getting together with Kyle, and now I'm wondering if that memory is to remind me it will take a lot of time for him to change, that he needs a *lot* of work. Is that hope? Is it possible God will do that for me? Kyle? His (God's) glory? I know it is; I just need the faith to say He *will* do it. Oh, how I want more faith and peace in this. It will happen eventually. God will give me a sign somehow, some day.

9/2/16

I'm spending this weekend with my sister Jennie and am waiting at the park for her to come home. I feel led to write. I'm receiving peace off and on in the midst of my emotions.

9/4/16

Yesterday at Jennie's church and today at my church, I noticed a theme. There are two key words recurring to me lately: conflict and peace. Handling conflict appropriately to reach a resolution and living at peace with others. Even if they continue to hold a grudge, at least we did our best and will leave God to handle the rest by prayer. I know I did right with Kyle in handling that conflict. I'll try my hardest to allow God to work in and through him in God's own time. I also need to be patient and just continue in prayer, even in tears I pray for Kyle. I think I'm still in love with him and am not sure it'll go away. As much as I want to be content as a single person and never desire to marry, I think that desire won't go away. For some reason, there's hope for Kyle's salvation.

On my way home from visiting Jennie this morning, I saw the sunrise. Something I love dearly. I drove down the interstate and praised God for the beauty of His skies, His works, and His love. I praised Him in this storm of crazy emotions. I cried aloud to Him for peace and *immediately* felt it! I laughed and felt chills as I sometimes do in His presence. He was there with me. He gave me peace and reassurance. Jennie reminded me, I have to be so lost in God, seeking Him, that a man will have to seek Him to find me. It's true.

God is faithful and while I'm waiting to see what He's trying to tell me in this season, I'll soon find out. This storm will pass and isn't permanent. I'll have a job. Praise God I found out today via email that we received tuition assistance for $2000.00 out of the $5409.00 for Damon's fifth grade. I'm grateful for His provision, grace, and kindness. He truly does take care of me and Damon. While others worry about money all the time, I do not. My bills are always paid, Damon continues to have a Christian education, and we always have all we need. I am content with God's provisions.

I don't know why I worry about not having a job since I am convinced God provides for us. I have an interview Tuesday for a position working with the homeless. Whether it's meant for me or not, I don't know at this time. I trust God will give me what's best. My anxieties and depression have lessened a little. I'm thankful for the prayers of my friends and church family to help me through this. I don't know why I write, but God leads me to it. Maybe I'll put it in an electronic format someday. Maybe I'll need these reminders in the future because my memory is bad.

LIFE LESSON

9/6/16

My gosh, where do I begin? I'll start with the repetition that may be God's hint to me. The book Jennie gave me, *You're Late Again, Lord!* [3] by Karon Phillips Goodman is extremely helpful for my current circumstance. She gave it to me at just the right time. It's about purposely waiting for God's timing. Working while waiting for God's answers to prayers and such. I've been writing in journals, working on my testimony in bits and pieces, as well as coming here to the trails to write and pray daily. Is that "work"? I felt another devastation to my heart and held in the tears. I'll get angry, and I can feel it coming. Maybe I did deceive myself in thinking it was God saying we are still meant to be; it's just the "wrong time." I don't know. I prayed for clarity and His presence arriving here (to the park).

I guess I'll see what comes of this. I'm hurting right now, all over again. After talking and crying, I prayed for God to help me know it's Him talking to me. I pulled out my *Busy Mom's Bible* [4] and turned to the "Thought Starters" page that stood out titled "Restore Your Relationships" between pages 438 and 439: "If you remember that your brother has something against you, go and be reconciled with your brother" (Matt. 5:23–24 NIV). Forgiveness from God coupled with responsibility toward the other person are key toward restoring relationships. In Jesus's eyes, broken relationships are always our responsibility. If someone has something against us, He calls us to go and make it right. If we have something against another, we're responsible to take the initiative to settle our differences—see Matt. 18:15. It's not always comfortable, but it is always the right thing to do. Do whatever it takes to restore the relationship. Do it because it pleases God and because your relationships will be richer for it." [4]

9/7/16

Now as I sit at the library reading my Bible, feeling led to finish the Old Testament, it started to *pour* outside. Heavy rain, thunder, lightning—God is here. It always feels like He speaks to me in the thunder. I feel comfort in storms, as long as I'm inside, of course. I went to my usual park to cry out as I often do. I hate being a pity party but need to vent all of this out. God gave me peace there, and while I walked to and from, I felt angry about Kyle. I don't want to love him or hope that he'll change because what if I'm let down?

I think God said on that trail, "Don't put your hope in him or trust in him, put it in Me! I'll work this out" (Psa. 118:8). Then as I was in the middle of an anxious thought, a squirrel jumped out and attacked me from behind. I shouted out of surprise as he was hiding in a tree stump where he latched on my side and jumped off. I have to admit, as angry and hurt as I felt while complaining that I can't tell if it's God talking to me or me deceiving myself, I did laugh. I think

He did that to distract me, and to make me smile. "You reap what you sow" (Gal. 6:7).

I think I just caught a revelation after thinking about my anger toward Kyle in regard to forgiveness. (He still hasn't expressed forgiveness toward me or apologized for his errors.) How long did it take for me to forgive others for the wrong they did—or moreover, what I thought they did? In the past, not only has the other person hurt me, but I did wrong and hurt them, too. I think of another ex and the mean things I said to him when we broke up and the wrongful gossip I spread at work. That went on too long.

Now years later, I reconciled with that ex, apologizing, and we are friends. The burden is lifted for both of us, and he asked me why, so I explained. The same goes for my best friend. I wanted to reconcile with her for years before I actually did but was afraid. Then I emailed her an apology, and we are best friends again and closer than ever. Wow, the realization. Is that what this is? You sow in anger and then you reap a waiting period of forgiveness and restoration? Kyle doesn't know any of that, as I hadn't in the past. Boy, he is way behind. Patience is key.

COMFORT IN LETTING GO

9/8/16

I feel I'm getting closer to peace in this situation. I can see it coming, but I know for sure I'm not there yet. Yes, there remains anger and hurt that he never apologized or took responsibility or accountability for his actions, but I have to remember that he is of the world. He is not a true believer or follower of Christ in the way I thought he was. He is not yet a man who has experience in life to show him what is truly good and what to appreciate. Oh, how I wish I could let go this instant—I just want peace. I want my feelings for him completely gone and eliminated as he had already done with me long ago.

In my car, it hit me—the love of Jesus is all I need. I heard it and have been told many times, but for some reason, it finally hit me. He loves me more than anyone else ever will. And Damon's love is enough, too. My child loves me despite my faults and imperfections. He cares and shows it. His love is an action. I also had the revelation that the Lord *is* preparing me for eternity. This life is temporary, and suffering isn't permanent. The peace I feel in God's presence will be permanent in my time to go from Earth. Wow. God's love is enough, and He gave me my child to show me a physical glimpse of that.

9/9/16

I recognize God is using this time of unemployment, feelings of devastation to the unanticipated outcome of my life, and waiting—to draw nearer to Him. I know He'll provide my needs and a job. I just need to be patient. I've been reading, writing, and working on my testimony bit by bit. Each day I'm "working." I'm trying to find ways to be productive in this waiting period. As I reread my first journal entry on 8/29/16, I took in the words "let it go and trust God."

9/10/16 (Prayer retreat notes)

I just received a revelation that the heart is deceitful; it is not good to follow your heart. Use your mind and logic. Listen to God; even if there are no red flags, pray to Him first. Ask the right questions and then wait. It sounds like things I already know. The only problem is, I don't act on it. I always tend to listen to my deceitful heart. Why did God lead me to this verse? Romans 8:25 (NIV) says, "But if we hope for what we do not yet have, we wait for it patiently."

I'm looking in Matthew again for scriptures on forgiveness and restoration. The page is open, and I turned to Matthew 18:21–22 (NIV): "Then Peter came to Jesus and said, 'Lord, how often shall my brother sin against me, and I forgive him? Up to seven times?' Jesus said to him, 'I do not say

to you, up to seven times, but up to seventy times seven.'"
Then, I went to the concordance of my *Busy Moms' Bible*
under the topic of Mercy and Reconciliation (page 1152).
[5] My mind picked up the thought to make an attempt to
restore with Kyle but I don't see him forgiving me or even
desiring to apologize to me or ask my forgiveness. Didn't I
do my part?

I put the work in the letter and the follow up. Why again?
Isn't it overkill? I thought I was waiting on him to be the
one to respond next, in his time, if ever. I don't want to
do this continuously, due to fear, anger, anxiety, bitterness,
sadness, and heartache. (Your Emotions, page 1157) [5]
Anger: Psalm 4:4, don't go to bed angry, search your heart.
Proverbs 14:17, a quick tempered man does foolish things.
Bitterness: Hebrews 12:15, see to it that no one misses the
grace of God and that no bitter root grows up to cause
trouble and defile many. "Be that example," He says (referring to the letter I wrote to Kyle). But God, how can I when
he pushed *me* away?

Proverbs 14:23: "All hard work brings a profit" is pointed
out as I peek in my Bible under my notebook. All of a sudden,
I think I may have to write another letter. I really don't want
to and am fearful of it. I don't know why there's fear, but it's
there. Proverbs 13:10 comes to mind now: "Where there is
strife, there is pride, but wisdom is found in those who take
advice." I don't even know what to write about.

My elder explained what I once thought: the constant "busyness" means Kyle is running from something. The other day, I thought I heard the Lord say He will humble Kyle. He has to come to a place where he'll have nowhere to turn but God. I think maybe the letter I might have to write will be in preparation for that? A guide? He has no one else to help lead him in the Lord. It doesn't seem it'll come from the type of church he belongs to, and I know it won't come from his family or friends. Am I really the only one to help?

I gave him my pastor and elder's numbers. Will he not call? Why me? Is it now? "Be that example." It's what I wrote in the other letter. I wanted to be a good example to him, and I failed. But God, he isn't for me. He's not there. He refuses to accept You; isn't that true? He's not a true believer and is a procrastinator, an excuse maker. He's always "busy" and "tired." He didn't even read the Bible verses I wrote in the first letter.

Last night I impulsively did something out of bitterness and anger. I immediately felt convicted and guilty that I shouldn't go against what God is doing by trying to sabotage things. I had a feeling it would've prevented God's work in some way. I don't know this for sure, but it's what I felt. Maybe I'll write a letter and see what happens. I'll know it's of the Holy Spirit if the words come as easily and smoothly with feelings of true peace as I write. If that's the case, then God's will be done. If not, I will tear it up. Romans 3:20

(NIV) says, "Through the law we become conscious of sin." He (Kyle) asked me, "What is sin?" One must know the law and God's commands to know what sin is. Romans 2:13 (NIV) tells us, "For it is not those who hear the law who are righteous in God's sight, but it is those who obey the law who will be declared righteous."

9/11/16

Wow. As I sit here at my park, prepared to do whatever God is leading me here to do, I'm in awe. I think I hit a realization. Deuteronomy 4:29–30 (NIV) says, "But if from there you seek the Lord your God, you will find him if you seek him with all your heart and with all your soul. When you are in distress and all these things have happened to you, then in later days you will return to the Lord your God and obey him." What then occurred to me was the last part in verse 30. I've not obeyed Him in the area of my biggest weakness. My weakness in sexual sin. Saying no until marriage and *sticking* with it! I am convicted prior to the sin, during the sin, and after the sin, yet I still do not have the self control to say no, or no more.

This is why I'm here. The suffering and heartache of it will continue until I do so. First Thessalonians 4:3–8 (NIV) tells me, "It is God's will that you should be sanctified: that you should avoid sexual immorality; that each of you should learn to control your own body in a way that is holy and honorable, not in passionate lust like the pagans, who do not know God; and that in this matter no one should wrong or take advantage of a brother or sister. The Lord will punish all those who commit such sins, as we told you and warned you before. For God did not call us to be impure, but to live a holy life. Therefore, anyone who rejects this instruction does not reject a human being but God, the very God who gives you his Holy Spirit." It doesn't matter if I pray for God to take my previously requested verbal punishment of it away, out of my promise to Him. He holds me to that promise I made and won't allow me to continue in it without the suffering to follow. He is God. It's His way, not mine. His command to obey Him.

This trial I am suffering is because God is saying "*No more.* I don't want you to suffer another heartbreak like this." The sermon in church today was focused on what the Bible says about humility in James 4. The worship songs reflected it also. It made me realize, as much as I hate being sensitive, soft hearted, caring, loving, and hurt too easily—other people pray for this in humility. Even males. To have a heart like God's isn't a bad thing. It's a blessed thing. I think I need that reminder all the time.

God says I'm finally listening. I really to want to obey Him; I always have. I'm just weak. I need to pray and seek Him daily and am now recognizing the true importance of it. One thing I did realize today—I felt bad about my anger toward Kyle, less bitterness. I recalled one instance toward the end of our relationship where he did show he cared in a small way. When I talked with my friend Sandy for hours while residing out there with him, he texted me late, saying if I was stuck somewhere and needed a ride, to let him know.

He didn't hate me then. I think that was the last Saturday I resided there. I was only focused on the negative things he did, such as talking poorly to me, putting me down when he was mad, locking me out of my home, talking negatively about me to his friends and family, isolating me, distancing himself, pushing me out and away, and was easily willing to sleep with a stranger a few days after I left. Those memories are what kept and keep me bitter, angry, hurt, confused, sad, and anxious. That one memory of the text I mentioned above lessened my bitterness and brought an understanding to light.

Philippians 4:8 (NIV) says "Whatever is true, whatever is noble, whatever is right, whatever is pure, whatever is lovely, whatever is admirable, if anything is excellent or praiseworthy, think about such things." If my thoughts are negative, I will end up feeling that way. I do now remember Kyle saying, "Think positive." At least he had that. Maybe if I focused on the positives, it will help me to forgive him easier, lessen the bitterness, anger and hurt. I have a lot of random things written down in various places, like I'm taking notes for something but I don't know what. Though

LIFE LESSON

I don't understand it now, I'm sure I'll see it later. God will reveal His purposes to me. He is good, forever faithful, and His love endures even to the likes of me. He sees our hearts and knows our potential. Be humble, or the Lord will humble you.

As I walked toward my car, I heard Him say to go to my spot on the rock back by the trail, so I went. There, He told me I need to forgive myself first, then forgive Kyle, and then I'll be able to let it go and trust Him. So, I spoke out afterward, thinking of my shortcomings. I forgave myself and then Kyle of his shortcomings. I was once where he is. Then I let it go and surrendered this to God. A burden was lifted.

One thing I forgot to write about that I realized a bit ago, is something I need to work on—my perception of the world. I noticed it while living up north being a stranger in a "foreign land." I was convicted I hadn't been loving others as I should. There's still good in the world and good people out there. I need to smile more at others, say hello, and so forth. I've been working on this since I first realized it but not hard enough. Even though the world is evil because it's led by the Prince of Darkness and people are deceived by him, I should respond lovingly.

I have a big heart and should *show* it more without fear of getting hurt continuously. I need to be a good example to *all*, not just a select few. The more I smile, the more I'm sure it'll become a habit instead of the look of sadness when I feel depression. Laughter is good for the soul. I really do need to find something I enjoy and do it more often.

ACCEPTANCE

9/12/16

While taking a break on my run on the trail, I found a spot by the water that stood out to me, and I was led to stop. A little branch looked just the right size where I could sit. It was peaceful and pretty. I thanked God for the blessings in my life right now and the work He's doing to help heal me. I feel a little more content and less bothered than I was before. I'm grateful for that. I cried and asked if He wants me to pray for Kyle because this is *still* an area which confuses me.

I prayed for clarity, understanding, and wisdom. I also prayed (in my own selfishness) for God to give me a sign that will help me know it's His voice I'm hearing and not my own. The heart is deceitful. My prayer was to help discern the voices I hear in order to hear His more clearly. I sat for a while. I argued with myself that I don't know why I was sure Kyle was the one and why this time was different than the rest because even in our hard times I knew and had peace. Then God took it all away. God gives and He takes away.

I was reminded of Job. Job then received even more than he had taken away after he realized God's goodness. I've always been led to the book of Job, mostly because of my homeless experience but now I see it can apply to various circumstances. I also reflect on the saying: "If you love something, set it free, and if it's meant to be, it'll come back to you." It popped in my head, but I always felt it wasn't true because the ones I loved never came back. Well that's not fully true because some would, and by then I knew they weren't meant for me because of the prior red flags and warning signs of their lifestyles or what have you. That's why I'm confused now. This time was not like the rest. I was *so* sure.

In my time by the water, I had what may be another revelation. Shelly came to mind as well as the conversation I had up north with Sandy, who wanted me to connect with Shelly about her faith, saying she's searching but keeps getting lost and is trying. That conversation convicted me of the judgements I had of her, based on what others told me about her and my experience meeting her. I also thought of the Thought Starters: Restore Your Relationships (pages 438–9) section in my *Busy Moms' Bible*. [6] Maybe it's meant for her instead. I plan to send her a prayer for her son as a basis to send her a message and explain the purpose of my writing. I pray it will be well received.

I can't pick and choose who I forgive, or who I show mercy to. God did say He would give me a sign, to let me know if it's Him I'm hearing or not. I don't know how or by what means, but I sure hope my simple mind will get it! I thanked God for His faithfulness, love, mercy, and help in this.

While at the library, I just sent a message to Shelly, and it ended up long. We'll see how it goes. I immediately received an email response from an employer wanting to set up a second interview and will get a call by the end of the week. The timing of this blessing comes right after sending Shelly the long message. That is most certainly God's approval! Praise God for His faithfulness and the hope we have in Him.

I'm surprised to see Shelly's negative reaction to my letter. I seemed to have angered her. Well, I did my part and asked forgiveness. Now I sit at my other trail on the lake, on my bridge, not sure why I was led here. I feel bad that Shelly took it wrong. I didn't intend to rile her up. I'm asking God what to do from here. He wants me to take things day by day. Don't worry about or focus on the future. That's what causes anxiety. He says I did my part. I did the best I could to apologize to her, which was all I could do. Leave the rest to Him.

If I want to hear Him and seek His guidance, I need to clear my mind and heart. He is in the wind. I sense it. The weather is perfect to be here now. I feel peace. I remembered apologizing to Kyle's mom, too, in a message. I wonder how no one seems to know or understand forgiveness. I didn't even do anything wrong in the sense of *really* wrong or unforgivable. I don't get it. "They're not where you are."

I was just nearly scared to death! First, an otter swam across the water to a tree, then a squirrel runs behind me with food in his mouth. I thought something was coming at me. Now, I see a tiny turtle swimming in the water. The wonders. Is God trying to tell me something? I don't know what it'd be. There is a lot of good, why have I been blind to it? I've been focusing on the bad since coming home. I see peace comes from recognizing the good in all this: my loving church and friends, Damon, my family, and our health. There's much to be thankful for.

Well, unfortunately, Shelly continued to respond negatively by attacking me. I had no choice but to temporarily block her after continuing to try to respond in a respectful and mature manner. It's unfortunate how people can be. Is that a wakeup call for me? I ended up praying for her. I feel their small town is lost. I'm saddened. I give up on working on anything up there. I did my part, I think. I don't understand why God wanted me to communicate to Shelly, especially knowing she would respond in the manner she did. I really don't get it. Yes, it hurt what she said, but I'm glad I can move on from this, knowing I did my best and was the better person. I hope that's not pride on my part. What a day—though it was quite beautiful out.

9/13/16

I just met with my mentor and am upset about how I'm doing all this work for what seems like no good reason. The outcomes are not how I anticipated, trying to reconcile with everyone up north. They just don't get what it means to be a true Christian—not a single one of them. My mentor said maybe they don't see it now, but in the future, they will recognize how to live a true Christian life (through what I'm doing). She says I'm being obedient to God.

All the while, I want to stop doing this work. It's discouraging. I want to give up, get over it all and move on. It hurts, and I want to forget the whole five months I spent with Kyle. I know wanting to run away from this is a pattern of old behavior. Addressing it like this is not. My heart says I want things to be how they were with Kyle, but then thoughts of eliminating all of it and forgetting him are what race in my mind. My mentor says I don't want the pain. That's true. I'm confused. I want to stop working because I don't know if I'm supposed to do what I've been doing and if it's really God or me deceiving myself. I hate the uncertainty! Why do I only feel convicted and certain when I meet with Him and pray, and not in times like now?

Yesterday after blocking Shelly, I felt a sense of relief that I did what I could out of humility, and it resulted poorly on her end. I felt good apologizing, and now I'm hurt and discouraged, after seeing her negative, hateful response. The Lord told me not to be afraid, He is leading me to what is right. I'm glad a friend reminded me yesterday of Psalm 40; it suits what's going on right now. I'm sitting here at the park in our spot. I have a few hours before getting Damon and decided to spend it with God since I crave His presence, direction, and peace. I need this daily.

He says, "You'll be blessed by this wait, and it'll give Me the glory. You'll experience joy again. The pain you feel will last a little bit longer. Remember the past? How I've brought you though those hurts? It made you stronger. What is it you truly want most? Search your heart and tell Me."

I then told God aloud I want a husband who seeks Him first and has a heart for God, a lifelong marriage where God comes first. That has been what I wanted for years and through experience—have doubted its possibility. Even now—after Kyle. I was deceived by him. God said before, not to put my trust in man but in God alone.

He also has a promise: Psalm 37, particularly verses 3–8 that say, "Trust in the Lord and do good; dwell in the land and enjoy safe pasture. Delight yourself in the Lord and He'll give you the desires of your heart. Commit your way to the Lord; trust in Him and He will do this. He'll make your righteousness shine like the dawn, the justice of your cause like the noonday sun. Be still before the Lord and wait patiently for Him. Do not fret when men succeed in their ways, when they carry out their wicked schemes. Refrain from anger and turn from wrath; do not fret, it only leads to evil."

My mind can't fool my heart's desires. God knows that desire. He placed it there. I can't wish or pray it away. "The husband for you needs to do much work to get to the place you're at. He must humble himself, be aware of his sinfulness, and repent to Me. Then I can begin My work in him. You must be patient."

In my doubts I cried aloud "Lord Jesus," and all of a sudden, I felt a cool wind blow and a chill, which resulted in me laughing and crying simultaneously, as I felt Him for a brief moment. How faithful and loving He is, even in my doubting sinfulness. God says to pray for them and to forgive them. For how they hurt me and let me down. Prayer is a powerful thing when done in faith. He wants me to pray for each one. "Trust in Me. I've got it all worked out already." It's difficult to humble yourself and admit wrong to someone else, especially if they did more wrong to you.

9/14/16

This is surely a day for praise! I went to the park to run the trail and possibly sit and pray but knew I'd do it later for sure. When pulling into the park, my favorite song was playing. I was singing along, smiling, feeling wonderful—and all of a sudden as I sang "highest praises," I was struck with the most unusual feeling I can't explain. I couldn't speak or think. I wanted to laugh and cry at the same time. I was in total awe.

I truly believe I felt His touch in that moment and then heard Him tell me to go to my spot (on the trail). I did, of course. I felt peace and joy. It seemed the worry was gone, and I continuously praised God and prayed that whatever work He wants me to do, I would do, even if it's hard and hurts. I need to be obedient. He's proud of me for stepping out and trusting Him and meeting with Him and building our relationship. I also prayed for those up north as He encouraged me to. I was reminded of where I once was, and how God can touch anyone's heart.

As I sit now at the other park by the lake, I feel Him in the wind. I always feel Him in the wind. A fish jumped out of the water. Oh, how I have such peace here. It's always beautiful when I come to this place. It's sunny, warm, windy, and peaceful, with no distractions. God told me to continue to focus on Damon—that is especially critical now. I've been helping with homework, which he appreciates, taking him out for ice cream, going on walks, and so on. This time off is really helping me learn a lot. I'm learning what's important. When I got home earlier, I received the call to set up the second interview. Praise God! I know He'll give me what's best in this time. I'll go where He leads and take what He gives. I'm overjoyed by His faithfulness. He truly does take care of us, even in the midst of chaos and heartache.

CONTINUED GROWTH THROUGH THE PAIN

9/15/16

I feel bad. Last night and this morning I felt anger. I hate when that happens. It may be coming from thoughts of the past. God says focus on Him and set my eyes on the present. He was at work then and is now—I set an example, and God is working on making the seed grow. How I wish I didn't doubt at all; it's hard to see such impossible people have changed hearts.

"Look at the apostle Paul. Look at you. Who is in control of all things? Fix your eyes on Me and continue to do My work—that is all I ask you. It's easier than you think. Don't focus on their shortcomings. Did you forget the miracles I'm able to perform? Cast your fears to me. Perfect love casts out all fear. Love. Don't hate. Don't be angry. Love in the way I do. Love your enemies. Love those who hate you. Remember that rosary? That's how it began. You are Kyle's rosary."

If only I could see it. But I know we hope in what we do not see. I don't know why I feel different today than yesterday. I'm ashamed of my anger and old feelings of worry, trusting less and doubting. I want the peace I had yesterday and faith and trust that God *is* working. I'm led again to the park by the lake to see what God wants me to do. For some reason, I feel He wants me to write another prayer—this time for Shelly. I don't know why I'm writing these prayers, but I'll do it. I felt the wind increase when I asked if it was Him talking to me. He says He wouldn't have me do this preparation work for nothing—there's a purpose in all of it. He says we will be restored. We will be friends again; he just has to get over his "anger hurdle." Not sure what that means.

9/16/16

"My child, I love you so. Everything will be okay; you'll see. I'm doing a marvelous work in your life, and you'll see the result of the wait—not only to draw nearer to Me, but to show that your difficult work won't be wasted. I'm well pleased with you. You're stronger than you think. You'll make it through. Your joy will be restored. Smile more; people love your smile, and it's a gift I gave to you. Always smile, practice it." (As a fish just jumped out of the water in front of me!)

The Lord is really here. It's been pretty windy, another beautiful day. I finished the book which the Lord says He gave to me for a reason. The impulsive decision I made to visit Jennie was for a purpose. We both shared our experiences, and saw the work God is doing. We are seeking God as our refuge, and I was blessed to see her example of writing prayers, reading the Word, praying, and encouraging me. God has a purpose. That book helped me understand my wait in this painful time of loss and drastic unforeseen circumstances. "Nothing is wasted. You'll see."

9/17/16

For some reason, I think I may type out all these journal entries but wonder why, since I can access my journals. I'm not sure if some parts of it will be included in my testimony. I suppose the Lord will reveal it to me. I'll just wait and continue to try to take things day by day. I've been appreciating the time spent with friends and family. I really do have many people that care about me. I'm reminded I need to be more like Christ and allow Him to work in me, as He works in us until the day of completion. That's my desire, to love others more, even if they hate me, to understand where they come from. I used to live as an unbeliever, I should know.

God's teaching me that while I hate having a big heart and caring too much at times, the world needs this desperately. It hurts more when I'm rejected, let down, abandoned, used, and so on, but maybe that's a sacrifice I have to make as an outcome of the love in my heart. I want to hide it and eliminate it but God says *no*. He uses it for His glory. I must be obedient and do His will, as I often pray "His will be done." I really am learning through this pain, aren't I? I can add that one to my story!

Lord God, can I please get over Kyle for good? That's on my mind right now. While I remember our meeting times where I pray and listen—I'm afraid. I feel I may be deceiving myself in this and end up disappointed. I think it all still hurts mostly because he didn't apologize yet, still has me blocked (on social media), and still acting as though this is nothing. Father, help me; it hurts. I try to turn this to You daily and feel the peace of it most times, but right now it hurts. Please have mercy and eliminate any feelings I have for Kyle, get me past this, and get me over it, so I don't care anymore.

Why all this work for him? He doesn't care. He just wants to live in the world and do as he pleases. He doesn't care about sin or doing the right thing. Please Father have mercy on me. This burden is too much! Is it possible to alter what God's plans are? If I want something different and act on it? If I'm not deceiving myself, and it is true that Kyle is for me, it'll just be awhile before he gets to the level he needs to be on. What if I'm so mad that I don't want it anymore? I can't wait forever to see if he changes.

If he doesn't change and I wait, I could miss an opportunity with a good man who'll treat me better. One who will actually show love with action, instead of just saying it. One who will love me for me and not be disappointed in who I truly am. One who will want to spend time with me and not be "too tired" to see me all the time. One who will work on the relationship equally with me and not against me. One who has his priorities in order, and above all, one who loves God and sets time aside for Him, placing all else under God. That may never happen.

I think when I get a job, I'm just going to have to set my life up as if there will be no husband. Even though before I said I was going to wait, not buy a house and get fully settled somewhere. But why? What am I waiting for? Something that may never happen? I have family, church, and friends. That's all I need next to God. Does that mean I have lack of faith? Lack of trust? Lack of hope? Yes, to all of the above.

As I sit by Lake Michigan on the rocks, getting bitten by flies, I'll continue to pray for help. I'm lost. And out comes the water works again. I'm done working for Kyle. I don't want to be obedient anymore. I don't want to have anything to do with him or think of him ever again. I'll try my best to eliminate him from my memory for good. Then I can move on. I'll never give my heart out to another man. Never will I go through this again. This cut was the deepest because I truly believed he would be my husband. But he isn't. Shame on me. Forget you, Kyle.

9/18/16

Today's sermon in church was on James 4:13–17 about not boasting of tomorrow because tomorrow is never guaranteed to us. Today is the day the Lord has made, and we need to set our sights on this day. We need to make sure we're ready when the Lord comes or when it's our time to go. We're a vapor compared to God's eternal plan. I sense another recurring theme: focusing on today and not worrying about the future or dwelling on the past. This morning, I heard a song on the radio and listened to the lyrics. I cried. I still hurt and have anger.

In focusing on the theme of today, I need to stop being angry. "In your anger, do not sin." Or "do not go to bed angry." Well I've done all that, obviously. I know I shouldn't. I'm out at the park again while the weather is nice. Won't be long until winter and my depression returns—the seasonal depression. My current depression is situational. I'll now sit and hope the Lord will have mercy and speak to me, as much as I don't deserve it.

He said to open to Matthew and I paged to chapter 21 and looked to verses 18–22 of "The Fig Tree Withers (NIV)." "Why do you doubt? Do you not see how everything is connecting together? I'm making it plain for you as you asked. This work is coming together. Aren't you paying attention to the repetition of messages? I'm telling you something as to reassure you. Do not doubt. Have faith in the work I can do with Kyle and do not doubt. My will prevails! Trust me! You will receive what you ask for; just have patience and wait for My time, not yours! My child, forgive him, even though he has not asked for it. Forgive him from your heart. That is the start of your healing. He'll come to you for forgiveness but you must forgive him first. He falls short, he sins, he doesn't understand because he does not yet have My Spirit in him since he has not asked. He's not ready at this moment, but he will be. Remember where you came from. Remember who you were. Before I softened your heart and convicted you of your sinfulness and opened your eyes. Do not doubt. Trust in Me."

TRUST

9/19/16

Today is another beautiful day. Earlier, I met up with a friend to go for a walk, and a thought came to mind having something to do with what he told me about the park I frequently go to. He said two girls were raped and murdered by what may have been a transient living in the woods. He wanted to tell me in April—as he knew I always go to this park but wasn't able to because he thought I blocked him on social media. I told him I didn't block him but had deactivated my account for a while around that time.

Interesting. I wonder if I did find out at that time, would it have prevented me from now going out to meet with the Lord as I've been doing? I don't have fear when I sit in His presence; it's when I'm away from it where I feel more cautious. I know God keeps me safe. I now sit closer to the edge of the trail, rather than further into the more isolated place, keeping my mace, buck knife, and phone handy. There's no one stronger than Almighty God, and He has protected me from many dangers. Seen and unseen. I'm glad to be reconciling with people.

9/21/16

It's raining out today. I sought shelter in the park instead of going to my trail. It's raining leaves, too—fall is almost here. That means my time coming out into nature to meet with God is coming to an end. I just read through some of my earlier writings in this journal and noticed a change in my feelings. They're slowly improving, and I'm slowly learning. There were a few good reminders in there, too, that made me tear up. I don't know what type of work to do anymore. I write down prayers now, which is something. My mind is distracted. I've been applying at other jobs here and there. God will provide.

I think at this point, my work with Kyle is done. There's nothing more I can do. I don't feel led to do any more, and if my previous writing is correct, I have to wait for him to get hold of me. I'm glad those feelings seem to be gone now. I feel more content—which is miraculous. It's been over a month now since I've been back home. I'll wait on God. "Await my instruction. I have not abandoned you. Time heals. Go to our place on the rock. I am continuing to work in your life. You'll continue to move up. Keep working on your relationships with others, be a good example, be patient, and be humble. Your work won't go unnoticed, even the tiny little details. Stop worrying. Trust in Me. Each circumstance brings you closer to who I want you to be. I didn't lead you here (to the rock) for nothing.

"I know you're uncertain and confused but take heart—I'll open your eyes. You'll see the miraculous works I will do. I'll cover you with My peace through this. Just keep waiting. You make a difference in people's lives—they recognize that. Your presence gives off My peace. I know you find that hard to believe, but I work through My children.

He'll recognize how valuable you are, my child. They always do after you're gone. You are of special value—you're not like other women. Don't become bitter. You'll love again, despite your current feelings about it. Someone will appreciate your heart, and while you don't believe it now, you'll see it one day, on the day I have prepared for you. You ask that I give you a sign in your heart, to validate My voice. I will show you."

Deep down, I think I'm to write about my experiences and put them into a book, though it's already in process. It's interesting how people's testimonies are brought about. I wonder what God's going to do with mine.

9/22/16

"There's a season for everything. The season is changing now from summer to fall. I feel those changes as well in my life. There's a time for laughter and joy and a time for sorrow and pain. I think I'm in transition now, just like the season. I'm anxiously waiting for an answer on this job, but I know God will provide at the right time. I'm not sure what He wants me to do, as it feels distant. I surrender my worries, depression, anxieties, burdens, and hurt to You, Lord. Please take them and give me Your peace today. May Your will be done. I know You're in control and will continue to take care of us. You'll provide a job for me.

9/23/16

Well, praise and honor and glory to the Almighty God! Yesterday, while about to run with Damon at the park, he told me my phone was ringing (as he kept it in his pocket). I got excited. It was the employer I waited to hear from, with a job offer, and the salary was going to be the highest it's ever been! I felt as if a giant burden was lifted and praised my Lord when I got off the phone. I had a feeling deep down, this was the one and am grateful God gave it to me. It's been my dream to work with the homeless, and now I have the opportunity. I'm now here at my spot, even though it rained and can rain again, but God deserves my thanks and gratitude over His works in my life.

This is one less thing to worry about, and I'm relieved. I don't know where we'll go from here, but I trust God will work it out for our best interest because I want to continue to place it all in His hands—for His will to be done, not mine. I feel bad that I always scare those big, blue heron birds away when I go to my meeting place—both here and the lake. They seem to often sit in the water near the place where I go. I wonder if they feel God's presence there, too. And those dang squirrels are always around me! I've got another week off before starting my new job—I wonder what the Lord wants me to do in the meantime.

I'll look at all this time off as a big vacation. I feel the wind blowing as I ask what He'd have me do. He says I'm falling behind and need to catch up on some things—especially my writing. I need to use my time to write. I'm worried I'll sound bitter since I last left off with Kyle in my "Life Lesson." God says He'll lead me. This is my purpose—to tell others of what God has done in my life. It will affect many as well as receive opposition, but that will be the enemy and I should not fear.

So, I sit on a bench at the lake, thinking about how I don't want Kyle anymore. It still bothers me, all that happened and how I failed to see he wasn't a true Christian. I know certain triggers get me to feel emotional. He's not good for me or my health. I want to move on. There's not even the slightest hint that he's changed or has the capability to change. He didn't do it with me, so why would he after the fact?

I think I need to seek a new church to find people my age. Maybe that's where I'll meet a man of God. But which one? "Don't work without Me." He doesn't want me, Lord. If You could please help me understand *why* You had me go through this. Why did I meet him? I'd like to understand. Why did all that happen out of the blue? Why did You lead me to go there and then come back? Why were there no red flags or warnings? Why, God, why? Why did You let me give my heart to someone else when I desperately never wanted to do that again? Why did you do it?

"What were you running from? Brad? That was your motivation. You sought shelter and protection from a man rather than Me." But You placed him in my life years ago. Then You let us meet years later. Why did You allow us to meet? I was ready to give up on him! This started before Brad and that incident. I think I'm going crazy having an argument in my head, thinking it's the Lord talking to me again. I'll pray for confirmation from God.

9/24/16

I feel a little more peace and contentment than the previous days. I seek refuge in You, Lord. May You be with me as I go through the upcoming new changes in life. Lead me in Your way, as it's always good and always best for me. The wind assures me You're here. I feel peace. I want to grow in You, Lord; help me to be an example. Help me in my new job. Let others see You in me. Praise and honor and glory be to You, Abba Father, for You are faithful and true. In the midst of my suffering and despair, you were with me and met with me whenever I sought you out in our meeting places. You comforted me and gave me Your peace. It is You alone who helped me get through this and blessed be Your Name!

"I am well pleased with you, My child. Before you were even brought about into this world, I had special plans for you and for Damon. People around you know there's something special and sense a goodness about you. See? Having a heart isn't a bad thing! I have much in store for you, more than you could ever imagine. You are special to Me. Continue to seek Me out, so no time is wasted. Keep working on your testimony. I know it's hard, but you can do it. Allow Me to work with you, and at just the right time, I'll place someone in your life to help see you through it. You may think you can't write, but you do just fine. You are human, you have a story to tell, and I'll receive the glory for it. Souls will be saved. Just keep writing."

How I'm grateful for the Holy Spirit.

PATIENCE

9/26/16

"Lord, I need Your peace today. For some reason, I suddenly feel anger at Kyle all over again. I keep having flashbacks of all the things he did wrong to me and how he *still* hasn't apologized. He may never do so, just like my other ex, Charles. Neither of them knows You, Lord. I need Your peace. Why can I not yet completely forgive him? Why does it take so long? It's been over a month and a half.

"Don't worry, My child. I'm working. I'm working. You just have to be patient. Healing is a process, it takes time. Remember the other times? Just focus on Me daily. Have no fear; cast your worries to me. I am doing wonderful things. I hear your prayers from the heart; that's why I asked you to write them—so you remember and see the work being done in its due time."

It's cold and windy at the park today. Leaves are falling more and more. God is here. I asked Him to meet me on the rock, and I feel Him in the wind. I wanted to start my day out here with Him before going on. I need His presence and peace because of my fluctuating emotions. I talked to an acquaintance about another church, but it has hundreds of members, which is intimidating. I prefer small groups and personal friendships, a family in Christ. "Just await My instruction." Abba Father, I love You and want Your will to be done in my life. Please don't let me go off the path and backslide or make any decisions that go against Your ways for me. Help me and lead me, my heavenly Father.

As I worked on my testimony some more, I read some of my previous journal entries from a few years ago and am surprised. I didn't realize I wrote what the Lord spoke back then, too! I can't describe the feeling I had reading through them, as they helped me to remember my turning to the Lord through the emotional roller coasters—as well as healing and the struggles I faced then, what I learned, and sometimes the repetition of them—even to this day. I read about my prayer for my ex Charles back in Madison when we broke up. Of course, now I see how bad he was for me. I wonder if that'll happen with Kyle. I know what he did was no good for me. I'll walk to our bridge here and see what He says.

"You can now see My purposes for you coming together, can't you? You need to complete My work before you can get comfortable." (It's really windy out.) "Even when you start your new job, you can continue to meet with Me like this as you're currently doing. There's always time. I'll heal you of your brokenhearted state. You just read how you got through it the other time. You're learning what's important. You're learning what a good relationship entails. Don't break your promise any longer, My child. I don't like to see you suffer. My purposes are for you. Your husband is being prepared. It will be like it was. That was a glimpse to show you your future. Have hope in Me; don't lose it. I love you dearly. You'll be at peace with this someday. The anger will die down, it always does—in time. Everything will work out perfectly. Trust Me." Oh the peace and assurance I feel right now. Wow. "Forgive Kyle. He'll come around."

9/27/16

I worked about three hours on my story today. I was on a roll, and things were coming together. It's difficult for me to write about what happened up north, but I know God is leading and helping me through it. I remembered how I thought he was the one and the signs God showed me throughout my stay. The confusion about all this is exhausting. Why can't I search my heart and see what my intuition says? There's always the deep down feeling I know something to be true, yet don't know 100 percent because I cannot see.

I had the same feeling about this job because it seemed too good to be true and a dream come true, but I didn't know I'd get it because I can't see into the future. It worked out with the job, but not with Kyle. Why am I confused? He's not the one. I was directed to write a list of reasons why he's no good for me. I should accept it as that, right? I'm getting closer to the closure part of this. I wonder when my story will be complete. Oh Lord, I pray You speak to me—even if it's just one thing, just one important thing You want me to know right now.

"Just continue to pray for My will to be done. If you want Me to tell you one thing, it's this: Be still and know that I *am* God. Don't trouble your heart over circumstances you cannot control. Be at peace and allow time to make all things come together. No rushing. Be still, My child."

9/29/16

I came to a realization in the midst of searching my Bible for answers. A divided heart strays from God, and we should have a whole heart dedicated to Him. While I know this, I don't act on it. Lord God, please help me to do this. Let my heart go to none but You. If anyone comes my way where I get tempted, please give him understanding and the same heart for You. On another note, I'm over forty pages in my "Life Lesson." I wonder how much longer it'll be until completion. God is good—through good times and the storms.

10/1/16

I'm thrown off course once more. We'll be moving again. Story of my life—I can't stand it. It's one thing after another, after another, after another. Things are continuously being taken from me. Things my heart belongs to. Lord, why more loss? Why more suffering? Why another move? It's only been seven months, and this is our fourth move. Is it a blessing in disguise? I don't know now, but maybe it'll be revealed in the future. We'll see. I never anticipated these last, well, the entire year of 2016 to be such a terrible year. I'm sure God would say to think of the positives, but it's hard when the negatives feel drastically overpowering.

I'm currently reading through the book of Proverbs and came across Proverbs 3:5–6 (NIV) that says, "Trust in the Lord with all your heart and lean not on your own understanding; in all your ways submit to him, and he'll make your paths straight." It's a familiar verse, but I think it's a hint I should trust God and not my own understanding of this dreadful year. He may be directing my path—this rocky, tumultuous, frustrating path.

10/16/16

I'm at the park on my rock. It's been a while because I've been busy moving things into storage, working, and making sure Damon does his school work. It's dark and cloudy, and it may rain, but I don't care. I want to be here with the Lord. I'll pray and see what the Lord says. I asked Him to meet me here, and He said, "You cannot know the future, my dear; it's too much for you. Just focus on right now and wait. You know you can trust Me, and I know the desires of your heart. I know what you truly want even when you're confused. You won't be disappointed. I've heard your prayers, and your plans are already in place and unfolding as we speak. Remain in Me, trust in Me, talk to Me, cry to Me, think of Me, and above all—wait patiently for the blessings I have in store for you.

"Do not sin or get tempted. I know your weaknesses, but you can prevent that area of sin in your life. That is why you suffered in the way you did—for that sin alone. Now you must wait again. Have My peace, take heart. I have overcome and will help you continually in your struggles. You've learned a lot and I want you to continue writing in your book. It will accomplish great things for the lost. Your experiences and lessons have great purpose and meaning; don't feel that it's wasted. Your tears are accounted for, and your pain is not hidden in my sight. You'll see. I love you My child. Just keep going and follow My lead."

10/30/16

I've been repeatedly thanking the Lord. Even though times are hard, and I continue to struggle in various ways, God is still good, and He is still in control. My life is a roller coaster, and all I desire is stability—at least for some years. Several years. I hate 2016. I wish I could eliminate this year from existence and forget it ever happened, but I know God won't let me forget. I don't know how I'll make it financially, emotionally, or mentally, but I trust God has my wellbeing in mind and He'll restore my brokenness somehow, some day.

11/13/16

Lord, please provide a home for us. I want us to be back on our own again. This whole year has been full of suffering, bad memories, heartache, moving, sadness, sickness, and loneliness. I just want it all to stop and the year to be over. Can You please let 2017 be a year of mercy rather than suffering? No more moving, no more new jobs, no more change, no more sickness and stress. Please have mercy on us and give us a break. Restore relationships, bring peace and healing, and give us a spirit of contentment and patience, Lord. I need help. I need You. Please have mercy. At times, I think death would be best, but I know better and don't want that. Maybe it's the depression creeping in again. Only the Great Physician can restore me.

11/14/16

I cried so much today. I don't understand why I'm sensitive and cry at the drop of a dime. I always wish the sensitivity would go away! I feel incompetent at my job. I'm not trained to deal with AODA or mental health issues. This is hard; my head hurts, and my eyes burn. "Why do you worry? I brought you here, I'll bring you through it. I am the Almighty God who sees you through all trials. Do not be discouraged. Do not let your heart break. Sensitivity is wonderful in My kingdom. There is none greater than a heart like Mine. Those residents appreciate you and love that you care and you listen. Be strong. Have faith. Take heart. I am with you through and through."

1/2/17

I'm already searching for a new job. The verbal abuse, threats, and lack of support from colleagues are becoming too much as I attempt to wait patiently for change. I don't want to go anywhere that's not in God's plan for me. I want a stable, fulfilling, low stress job that's decent with a livable income. Have mercy, oh God, and fulfill that desire. I don't know what to do or where to go. I praise You for always paying our bills and keeping us housed, fed, and healthy. "Everything will fall into place. Have faith and be strong. I'll work on your behalf, and you will win favor in the eyes of many. Your suffering in this season is almost done. Be joyful for what is to come!"

4/1/17

God told me to forgive. This is the theme today as I drove to the library. Kyle came to mind. I couldn't see why, believing he hasn't changed, but I heard God speak: "Do you know man's heart? His thoughts? How do you know he hasn't changed at all?" I'm convicted. I prayed for him last week some time.

PEACE

4/7/17

I'm on my bridge on this semi cold yet sunny, beautiful day. It's been raining almost daily for a while now, but it made the grass green! My view on the bridge is all brown, even the water, but God is here! I've not felt depression all winter! I feel stronger than ever before. I see a little bird on a tree and am reminded how the Lord takes care of each little bird. I don't know why my heart is still confused about Kyle, but I'm at peace with everything. My heart longs to be up north, but maybe it's for a different purpose, I don't know.

"My daughter I'm pleased with you. Look at how much progress you've made, how much you've grown. Those hardships weren't permanent, see? You are special. That screeching hawk is for you. I know you love them!" The chirping birds remind me of the season of change from gloomy winter to blooming, beautiful spring and hope of a wonderful future. A reminder that God is in control.

"Your heart has changed. Remember how it used to be? I can make all things new. Keep praying for him. His heart will change. Don't doubt Me. He's reflecting during this time. I've got this!" What a great Abba I have. God is good. "Just keep writing your story. Others will want to hear it. I'll guide you."

Now that you've made it through those lengthy journal entries, I'd like to conclude this chapter with a side note.

It wouldn't be until February 2019 when I came across an article describing common emotions people feel in a narcissistically abusive relationship. It provided several examples of a narcissistically abusive person's behaviors. While reading through them, I realized many of these traits were identical to Kyle's behaviors toward me. It might explain those fluctuating emotions and overwhelming sense of confusion I experienced in that season.

I thanked God for allowing me to stumble across this article because even after a few years, I remained confused about what transpired. It helped me to officially let go of this disturbing circumstance which kept me in chains for too long. I've included the link in my Recommended Readings page toward the back of this book if you'd like to read more about it.

11

SPIRITUAL WARFARE REQUIRES DILIGENT PREPARATION

While exploring employment options, I prayed to be led to the right position. With this task being a recurrent part of my life, I was an expert job seeker. I applied for several positions, and one in particular stood out to me. It entailed working with people who were homeless and suffering from AODA (Alcohol and Other Drug Abuse) issues. For years, I desired to have an opportunity to serve this population, so I decided to focus on this prospect. It involved a brand new program, beginning on October 2016 in a nearby city. I praised God for this new program, a blessing to those who currently slept in the streets. It appeared to be the perfect job because I exhibit compassion and empathy toward those who sleep in the streets.

I scheduled both phone and in person interviews with the affiliated agency. I briefly explained my personal encounter with homelessness, which led to my interest in taking advantage of this opportunity. In addition, I described my lack of experience working with persons who suffer from AODA and anticipated training and support in that area. Following the interview, I received an offer of employment. I was told I presented myself in a way that's not condescending or superior and appeared to have a kind personality. Those qualities were emphasized in the job description. Another fresh start.

On November 30, 2016, I received shocking news regarding Damon's father, Thomas. His family reached out to tell me Thomas passed away, and it appeared to be related to a drug overdose. He was only thirty four years old. I wondered what kind of effect this would have had on Damon. Damon and I cried together upon hearing the news. My response caught me by surprise, due to the nature of our previous relationship. There were nights I cried myself to sleep. Tears flowed incessantly, and I didn't understand why.

Damon never had the opportunity to meet Thomas face to face, and I felt guilty for it. I wanted to wait until Damon became an adult before potentially allowing them to meet. The sole reason for this decision was for our safety. It was unfortunate things couldn't be different. Around this time, I learned Damon had not only audio hallucinations, but visual hallucinations. He heard voices and saw faces or shadowy figures. Those are worldly terms, but I know they truly involve spiritual warfare. "For our struggle is not against flesh and blood, but against the rulers, against the authorities, against the powers of this dark world and against the spiritual forces of evil in the heavenly realms" (Eph. 6:12 NIV).

On December 7, 2016, I wrote down what Damon told me as he described when it began, according to his recollection. The reason I wrote it down was to capture details in the event they may be relevant at some point in time:

> Over the last few months, Damon talked about hearing things. I started to pay more attention to this, connecting it with Thomas's experience in hearing voices (what I believe may have been schizophrenia or multiple personality disorder). He said he first heard voices when we lived near Madison from 2013–2014. There was only one instance in that town. He also heard voices a few times when we lived in the apartment in Racine from 2014–2016 and a few times at Mom and Dad's house. The first time I recall him bringing this up before paying any attention, was when we were in the car leaving Mom and Dad's. He said he heard someone tell him to do something bad. It was in his head and sounded like the devil (deep/scary).

When I asked him a few days ago if the voices tell him to do bad things he said no, but once they said to steal money. He doesn't always know what they say because it's in a different language or languages. The one time it told him to steal was in English. So far, while living here (with a friend), he heard a voice maybe two or three times. He doesn't hear it at school or church, and usually it's in bed. It hasn't been anywhere else with the exception of the car as explained above. There are no conversations in his head, just one voice at a time, and each time sounds different. They sound scary sometimes but not all the time.

On another note, he now tells me about seeing faces. Sometime in October 2016, he told me when he was in bed, he saw faces under the blanket. They were not scary, and he didn't recognize them. No voices. On December 6, 2016, he told me he saw a big hand at the door as well as a face under the blanket. He still didn't recognize it. When he got up, he saw part of a person's stomach by the door. He said he only sees things in this home (our friend's house), as well as faces when he walked in the hallway or by the door in his bedroom at the Racine apartment. They were sometimes scary to him.

He said when he's by me he doesn't see them, and he tries to get Misty (our cat) to help comfort him. After school today (12/7/17), he told me something scary. I'll backtrack to say there was something I prayed for days ago, out of feelings of guilt. When we found out Thomas died, the night I cried many tears, I asked God if Thomas could see Damon since he never got to meet him in this life. I felt bad. I asked God to be merciful and to do this just once.

What Damon told me today was something I hadn't mentioned to anyone. When I asked Damon what the people he sees look like, he said they're men, not women. One was "white like me," one was red like a Native American, and one was black. I asked him to describe the black man, and he described him as tall, an adult, short hair, and no facial hair but not a child. Damon didn't recognize him. He wasn't an old man, Damon was unsure if he was my age. The man didn't say anything to Damon but just stood at the end of the bed looking over by Damon. The description Damon gave was how I think Thomas looked.

When Damon sees faces, he doesn't hear voices, and when he hears voices, he doesn't see anything. He says he's getting annoyed by this and wishes he didn't see or hear anything. It's not troubling but more annoying. Damon just confirmed the man didn't look like Thomas's picture.

I asked Damon detailed questions about the things he saw and heard, as I wondered if he somehow had a connection to the spiritual world. He said he wondered if I saw them, too, but when he realized I didn't, he became frightened. The only time he wouldn't see anything was with me, at church, at school, or when he had the Bible with him in bed. It began to make sense why he was always afraid to sleep alone since he was a toddler. I often told him there was nothing to fear because God is always with us and has ultimate power over the enemy. I insisted he be a "big boy" and sleep in his own bed. As he got older, I encouraged him to sleep with the Bible for comfort.

Up until this point, I brushed it off, assuming he had a bad dream or saw something scary on television. I had no idea what he was actually experiencing. I stopped asking questions when he became uneasy talking about the images he saw. He didn't want to think about it and I didn't want to traumatize him. He often asked where my Bible was to keep at his bedside. Anytime I took my Bible off the stand, he immediately noticed and asked where it was. He wanted to sleep with it near him. I was blessed knowing Damon put his trust and faith in the Lord to protect him, knowing God's Holy Word would keep him safe.

Spiritual Warfare Requires Diligent Preparation

I asked several people to pray for Damon. If this was going to be a part of his life, I wanted him to be prepared and to cope with it effectively. Not long after the prayer requests, I asked Damon if he continued to hear or see anything. He said no, and I praised God. I explained only God could do that for him.

On January 12, 2017, I wrote about an unusual experience following Damon's report of not hearing voices or seeing images:

> This morning while taking a shower, I prayed for Satan's evil spirits to be cast out of my work place. Evil runs rampant there! When I woke Damon up for school, he said, "I just had the weirdest dream. You, me, and Misty were in the house, and you were telling an evil spirit to get out, and it was screaming and went out. Then, it made some weird noises like a trumpeting sound after it left." He didn't see the spirit; he only heard it and knew it was evil because of how it sounded. Wow!

I couldn't believe my child was somehow connected to this prayer and saw it himself in a dream. What made this prayer distinct from the rest were elements of strong confidence, great power, and a high level of faith. I wished I could pray like this all the time. I fell short in the faith department at times but knew it continued to strengthen as time went on.

Damon witnessed my increasing faith as we experienced life together. I hoped my faith would be an inspiration to him.

After obtaining employment, my next goal was to search for a home. I received a flyer in the mail from my bank encouraging me to stop in and find out what type of programs I'd be eligible for as a first time homebuyer. I was tired of what appeared to be an endless cycle of relocation. I craved stability. I can count at least twenty places I lived between the ages of nineteen and thirty three (minus shelter stays and sleeping outside).

In the previous year, I went to my bank to conduct a transaction, and the teller asked if I thought about buying a home. The thought crossed my mind, but I never knew where to start. I also didn't know if I'd be able to afford it. The lender said based on my numbers, I was preapproved. He referred me to a realtor, but none of the homes felt right. I decided to hold off until it was the right time.

That experience came to mind upon receipt of this flyer, and I wondered if it was a sign. There were several things I took into consideration. People often told me I shouldn't throw money away to pay someone else's mortgage. Additionally, a mortgage payment is often cheaper than paying rent. I knew apartment living wouldn't hold me down, but if I had a house, I'd be tied down. It'd help provide the stability I craved, so I decided to give it a try.

As the process ensued, everything seemed to fit together perfectly this time around. A friend of mine highly recommended her realtor, so I gave her a call. When I reviewed various homes in the area, one continued to stand out, and I wasn't sure why. It was the perfect fit for Damon and me, even though it was slightly outside the price range. When we toured the home, I sensed deep down this was the one. We looked at other houses to explore other options, but none felt like this one.

Damon and I happily chose this house that matched our needs. My lender and realtor were nothing short of excellent, and I thank God for placing them in my path. The closing date was set for February 10, and we were excited to be one step closer to owning our own home. Little did I know life was about to throw me another curveball, which would clearly test my faith in God.

Early morning on January 25, 2017, my supervisor and the program administrator met with me in my office and closed the door. They proceeded to say I wasn't a good fit for their program and wanted to do a "mutual termination." My supervisor said they feared for my safety and worried about me being alone with the residents. Since both of them were rarely ever present, they could only receive information from my colleague.

The residents in the program thought highly of me and often expressed appreciation about the work I did and my genuine concern for their wellbeing. Yes, it was an *extremely* unsafe environment and both my colleague and I commented about the need for something to be done about it. Unfortunately, nothing was ever done. Threats and violence only worsened. The information management provided didn't make sense as a valid reason for termination, and I didn't know what to say. I respectfully chose not to defend myself. They provided a deadline of one month to find employment elsewhere.

I was shocked. I'd *never* been let go from a job before. With God being omniscient, I wondered why He allowed this to happen, knowing I was about to close on a house. I wondered what He had in store and accepted this termination as part of His plan for something greater. In that moment, I realized how much my faith had matured. I knew God wouldn't leave me hanging. Anxiety and depression used to naturally surface the instant something life altering occurred. This time was different. None of those symptoms surfaced.

Once again, it was time to search for employment elsewhere. It was refreshing to see immediate responses from agencies requesting interviews. I wanted to direct my focus more on employment in a Christian organization where I could freely talk about my love for the Lord without resistance from management. I recalled a discussion with someone at church who informed me about a Christian organization in a nearby city that served the homeless. After reviewing the website, I decided to fill out an application and submit my resume and cover letter. Their schedule was different from what I was accustomed to. Second shift hours including weekends weren't appealing at all, but if it meant doing God's work, I was willing to make the sacrifice.

During the interview, I was astonished to see how different this organization was from others I worked for. What made this place stand apart from the rest was that the interviewers began our meeting with prayer. The other recognizable difference was the love and encouragement employees showed for one another. I sensed this was what God had in store, and peace entered my heart. I knew I had to search no more. It didn't take long to recognize God's purposes at this point. My past experiences and struggles as a single parent were key in relating to the mothers who sought shelter here. I had opportunities to speak about how God changed my life for the better.

One thing I didn't see coming was a sin problem of mine that needed to be addressed. The Lord was going to work in my heart to correct this sin and teach me a new lesson! I knew it needed to be addressed but never put forth enough effort to properly deal with it. My sinful struggle involved my view that (most) people's kids are spoiled and ungrateful. I wanted nothing to do with them. Sad, isn't it?

It had been thirteen years since I last worked with children. As time went on with my new job, my heart began to open up to them. I was finally comfortable working with children, showing love and encouragement and displaying patience and kindness.

Sometimes, little ones ran up to hug me out of the blue. I received coloring pages, as well as a handwritten note from a young girl saying "Ms. Kristina, I love you Ms. Kristina." Babies smiled at me all the time. Some children complimented me and asked, "Why are you so nice?" A teenage girl told me I was her favorite employee. God performed a great miracle. How did I never see this before?

In the midst of learning new lessons, something unimaginable happened to escape my notice. Winter was coming to an end, and spring was right around the corner. Normally, I dreaded this time of year because my depression would hit its peak. This time, I felt different—on the inside. Indescribable peace engulfed me, even in stressful times. Joy filled my heart more than ever before. The Lord became the center of my attention on a much more intentional basis, which led to the increased joy. I reflected on His faithfulness through various tribulations and began to understand each hardship was only temporary.

Once I realized depression was gone, I stood in amazement, knowing only Jehovah Rapha ("The Lord who heals") could take it away. I lived with depression for so long, I couldn't remember what it felt like not to have it. If you look back to my journal entry for 8/29/16, you'll see this was an answered prayer. It's God's response to my request of having *continuous* peace. Don't get me wrong, I still experienced moments of sadness, anger, frustration, and confusion, as they are all human emotions. The difference is the depression, which led me to feel miserable, lonely, unmotivated, self conscious, doubtful, fearful, anxious and discouraged, was no longer present in my mind and my heart.

Another change occurred as well. My interest in reading slowly came back. Once I finished college, I was set I wouldn't pick up another book for many, many years! I must have had a long enough break because I came across a book that caught my attention involving spiritual warfare. My prayer life was already in the process of change, especially after the morning when Damon said he had the dream about me telling an evil spirit to leave. I started to pray out loud, with stronger emotion. I focused more on demonic influence and spiritual attacks. I always prayed in the name of the most holy Lord Jesus. I don't know where this determination came from, I just started doing it.

Around this time, I was given a gift—a spiritual warfare devotional. It seemed God was trying to tell me something through recurring signs. Much of it pointed to Damon. After I told my supervisor about his experiences, she told me something important was going on, and I needed to keep him bathed in prayer. There's something about him that's threatening to Satan. While I don't know what it is just yet, I know it'll be revealed someday. I continued to encourage Damon in the Lord, reminding him to rely on God's peace and protection. I emphasized that Satan has no power and only tricks us into thinking he does.

I never saw myself as a teacher, or someone who had anything important to say. I often look to those who are older and wiser, yet by God's grace, I too am maturing. I long to help others see God's truth and use my experiences as an example to show how God is present in all details of our lives. It's extremely critical to fix our eyes on the Lord when we're being attacked by the afflictions of this world. Prayer is a powerful tool we have against the enemy. I want to include a few lengthy Bible verses since I'm on the topic of prayer and demonic influence (part of the first one was included in my Introduction):

> Put on the full armor of God, so that you can take your stand against the devil's schemes. For our struggle is not against flesh and blood, but against the rulers, against the authorities, against the powers of this dark world and against the spiritual forces of evil in the heavenly realms. Therefore, put

on the full armor of God, so that when the day of evil comes, you may be able to stand your ground, and after you have done everything, to stand. Stand firm then, with the belt of truth buckled around your waist, with the breastplate of righteousness in place, and with your feet fitted with the readiness that comes from the gospel of peace. In addition to all this, take up the shield of faith, with which you can extinguish all the flaming arrows of the evil one. Take the helmet of salvation and the sword of the Spirit, which is the word of God. And pray in the Spirit on all occasions with all kinds of prayers and requests. With this in mind, be alert and always keep on praying for all the Lord's people. (Eph. 6:11–18 NIV)

If God is for us, who can be against us? He who did not spare his own Son, but gave him up for us all—how will he not also, along with him, graciously give us all things? Who will bring any charge against those whom God has chosen? It is God who justifies. Who then is the one who condemns? No one. Christ Jesus who died—more than that, who was raised to life—is at the right hand of God and is also interceding for us. Who shall separate us from the love of Christ? Shall trouble or hardship or persecution or famine or nakedness or danger or sword? For I am convinced that neither death nor life, neither angels nor demons, neither the present nor the future, nor any powers, neither height nor depth, nor anything else in all creation, will be able to separate us from the love of God that is in Christ Jesus our Lord. (Rom. 8:31–35, 38–39 NIV)

If you fully obey the Lord your God and carefully follow all his commands I give you today, the Lord your God will set you high above all the nations on earth. All these blessings will come on you and accompany you if you obey the Lord your God. The Lord will grant that the enemies who rise up against you will be defeated before you. They will come at you from one direction but flee from you in seven. (Deut. 28:1–2, 7 NIV)

It was mid September 2017 when Damon and I went out for a walk at our favorite park. He wanted to tell me about recent dreams he had, explaining them as "end of the world" type dreams. I related to him by confirming I experienced similar visions in the past. He proceeded to tell me what happened in one of his dreams. He was at a train station when all of a sudden, he heard everyone scream. He turned around and saw a lightning bolt go through them, and they exploded into dust. After he boarded the train and it started to depart, the lightning bolt came and went right through him. He exploded into dust and turned into a spirit.

He looked around as he slowly floated up into the heavens where he saw God sitting on a bench. Damon gave Him a hug and felt happy. As this happened, Damon's friends saw him in his spirit and asked where he was going. Damon replied, "To heaven," and said goodbye to them. This was the end of his dream. I was amazed. I told him the Word says Jesus will come like a thief in the night (2 Pet. 3:10; 1 Thess. 5:2). He responded "Oh yeah, like a lightning bolt" (Mat. 24:27)!

> But about that day or hour no one knows, not even the angels in heaven, nor the Son, but only the Father. As it was in the days of Noah, so it will be at the coming of the Son of Man. For in the days before the flood, people were eating and drinking, marrying and giving in marriage, up to the day Noah entered the ark; and they knew nothing about what would happen until the flood came and took them all away. That is how it will be at the coming of the Son of Man. Two men will be in the field; one will be taken and the other left. Two women will be grinding with a hand mill; one will be taken and the other left. Therefore, keep watch, because you do not know on what day your Lord will come. But understand this: If the owner of the house had known at what time of night the thief was coming, he would've kept watch and wouldn't have let his house be broken into. So, you also must be ready,

because the Son of Man will come at an hour when you do not expect him. (Matt. 24:36–44 NIV)

Our conversation was a great reminder about the need to be prepared for Jesus's second coming. I must continue to be obedient to God's will. I must proclaim the truth of the gospel to a world full of lies and deception. I mustn't be ashamed to say His holy Name in public places. Resistance and persecution are inevitable in the life of a Christian, but Jesus gives His followers the strength to endure it.

12

THERE'S NOTHING TO FEAR IN TRUSTING A SOVEREIGN GOD

Throughout the summer of 2017, I read through my journal entries for two purposes. One was to reflect on what the Lord said to me. The other was to see if I could use anything for my testimony. I knew God wanted me journal for a reason, I just had to piece it together. At one point, I came across an entry written on 9/26/16: "*I talked to an acquaintance about another church, but it has hundreds of members, which scares me and is intimidating. I prefer small groups and personal friendships, a family in Christ. God told me, 'Just await My instruction.'*" The reason I reached out to him was because I considered switching churches, hoping to meet more people my age.

From the time I wrote the entry up until this point, I felt a nudge in my heart, primarily during Sunday services. There wasn't anything wrong with the church we belonged to, I just wondered if it was now time to switch. The Lord's response to wait for His instruction became clear. I decided one Sunday to attend the church that was placed on my heart. It was scary at first, but their service was identical to the one we were accustomed to over the last nine years. The only difference was the number of people who attended. A *great* difference. A few weeks later, I made the decision to switch for good.

The hardest part was letting my elder know. I felt so bad, it literally made me sick. Thankfully, the Lord helped me through this anxiety ridden transition. The sermons were topics I needed to hear in relation to what I was going through. It confirmed yet another way God speaks to His children—through sermons.

You're going to notice a theme here. A theme of change that would take me from where I previously landed to new places. God started to tug at me again to reveal what it was He wanted me to do. It's interesting to see how He works when you pay attention. This was going to be a season of difficult choices, but I knew who was in control.

There were instances at my job where I was able to minister to those who were hurting and going through troubling circumstances. My personal experiences were used to glorify God, which in turn helped me relate to the mothers and children who sought shelter and hope. I provided encouragement and pointed them to the One who could open doors and help them overcome challenges. While the task at hand was quite difficult, I knew it was meant to be. God placed me here to do His work.

It was also during this season when things became stagnant. My work schedule prevented me from having a personal life. I couldn't spend time with Damon or help him with homework. There wasn't much opportunity to meet with the Lord on a regular basis. I didn't burn stress off with exercise. I was just going through the motions. Symptoms of burnout resurfaced because I wasn't participating in self care. I hadn't been praying as fervently as before, which is highly critical to make it through the hard times. I put prayer on the back burner and suffered the consequences. With the way things were going, there was no way to get around this stagnancy.

I realized Damon and I weren't going to have any days off together once he started school after Labor Day. When I continued to review my journal while working on this book (9/14/16 and 9/22/16), I read what the Lord said about how important it was to spend time with him at this time in his life. He was going to be a preteen. To make matters worse, I found out my Sunday work schedule was going to change again. My hours would switch from 1 to 9 p.m. to 11:30 a.m. to 7:30 p.m., which meant we wouldn't be able to go to Sunday service anymore. Church was a part of our routine from the time Damon was born! I didn't know what to do. It was hard accommodating to this employer's schedule. I was accustomed to having weekends off and first shift hours for ten years.

Once again, I had second thoughts on whether or not social work was the right fit for me. I was sick and tired of not knowing what my purpose was regarding employment. I loved helping people, but it was too emotionally, physically, mentally, and spiritually draining. I was only at this job for six months. What was wrong with me? I reflected on a thought which occurred months prior. Was it possible God moved me around so frequently for the sole purpose of pointing people to Christ as best I could? I couldn't understand how I thought each place was where I was meant to be, yet I rarely lasted long enough to celebrate a one year anniversary!

Coincidentally, God had a message he wanted me to hear. I listened to a sermon one Sunday involving the topic of work. Work became cursed once Adam and Eve brought sin into the world.

> To Adam he said, "Because you listened to your wife and ate fruit from the tree about which

I commanded you, 'You must not eat from it,' Cursed is the ground because of you; through painful toil you will eat food from it all the days of your life. It will produce thorns and thistles for you, and you will eat the plants of the field. By the sweat of your brow you will eat your food until you return to the ground." (Gen. 3:17–19 NIV)

During the sermon, it was explained going from one job to another in the hopes of finding happiness would only lead to disappointment. Switching jobs isn't necessarily a bad thing, but you need to ask yourself why you're doing it. It had me thinking on a deeper level. I spent my day off at the library and heard the Lord give me an instruction. He had two tasks for me. The first was to send an email to my new church to inquire about any resources involving publishing a testimony. The second was to email a distant acquaintance, who was placed on my heart to see how she is doing.

I wondered, *Why her*? She used to attend our old church years ago. She hadn't spoken to me in a while, and though I didn't understand why God wanted me to send her a message, I did it anyway. To this day, she never responded. After sending the email, her husband John came to mind. I recently applied for a manufacturing job and remembered he worked there. For some reason, the company stood out to me, so I eagerly awaited a response from them. When I have a gut feeling about something, purchasing our house for example, I follow through with what my gut is telling me. The easiest way I can explain it, is I had a good feeling about it.

I later emailed John telling him about the application and asked how it was, working there. The following day, I received a phone call from HR to schedule an interview, and I was eventually offered employment. God knew I wanted to get out of social work, and He answered my prayer in His grace. Remember when I said it seemed my life had become stagnant? Out of the blue, I came across a new opportunity where I could be a positive encouragement for someone in need. Toward the end of June 2017, I found out someone I knew was incarcerated. He asked a relative to reach out to me, saying I was "a good Christian woman and strong in the Word." He was losing his faith and needed support.

My immediate thought was God had a purpose in this. Then, I wondered, "Me? A good Christian woman? Out of all the people he knows, he requested to hear from me? I'm not *that* knowledgeable of the Word!" Humility has become a part of who I am, if you couldn't tell. "Do not think of yourself more highly than you ought, but rather think of yourself with sober judgment, in accordance with the faith God has distributed to each of you" (Rom. 12:3 NIV).

I had an opportunity to use personal examples of how I grew in my relationship with the Lord. As we exchanged letters,

I was led by the Holy Spirit to certain scriptures as I paged through my Bible. It proved helpful when certain things needed to be said, especially when it came to explaining conviction of sin. My sermon notes were also helpful resources. It was good to see he was seeking the Lord in this dark time of his life. I felt led to be supportive through letters and visits. I wanted to show the love of Christ and encourage him to keep going and to not lose faith.

This reminds me of a time when I worked at the Christian based homeless shelter. We spent one of our all staff meetings focusing on spiritual gifts and took a spiritual gifts survey to see what our top three gifts were. It was helpful to learn and understand how I relate to others. I'll quote descriptions of my top three gifts taken from a spiritual gifts test website. I believe it provides an accurate description of my heart. If you have time, I encourage you to do the same. It may help reveal a God given purpose for your life.

1) Faith: The spiritual gift of faith is not to be confused with saving faith. All Christians have been given saving faith (Eph. 2:8–9), but not all receive this special gift of faith. The Greek word for faith in the New Testament is *pistis*. It carries the notion of confidence, certainty, trust, and assurance in the object of faith. The gift of faith is rooted in one's saving faith in Christ and the trust that comes through a close relationship with the Savior. Those

with this gift have a trust and confidence in God that allows them to live boldly for Him and manifest that faith in mighty ways. In the Bible the gift of faith is often accompanied by great works of faith. In Acts 3:1–10 we see this gift in action when Peter sees a lame man at the Beautiful Gate and calls on him to stand up and walk in the Name of Jesus. Jesus said even a small amount of this faith could move mountains (Matt. 17:20; 21:21). Paul echoed this truth in 1 Corinthians 13:2. The Holy Spirit distributes this gift to some in the church to encourage and build up the church in her confidence in God. Those with the gift of faith trust that God is sovereign and He is good. They take Him at His Word and put the full weight of their lives in His hands. They expect God to move and are not surprised when He answers a prayer or performs a miracle.

2) Mercy: All Christians are called to be merciful because God has been merciful to us (Matt. 18:33; Eph. 2:4–6). The Greek word for the spiritual gift of mercy is *eleeo*. It means to be patient and compassionate toward those who are suffering or afflicted. The concern for the physical as well as spiritual need of those who are hurting is covered by the gift of mercy. Those with this gift have great empathy for others in their trials and sufferings. They are able

to come alongside people over extended periods of time and see them through their healing process. They are truly and literally the hands and feet of God to the afflicted. The Holy Spirit gives the spiritual gift of mercy to some in the church to love and assist those who are suffering, and walk with them until The Lord allows their burden to be lifted. The gift of mercy is founded in God's mercy towards us as sinners and is consistently expressed with measurable compassion. Those with this gift are able to "weep with those who weep" (Rom. 12:15) and "bear one another's burdens" (Gal. 6:2). They are sensitive to the feelings and circumstances of others and can quickly discern when someone is not doing well. They are typically good listeners and feel the need to simply "be there" for others.

3) Exhortation: The spiritual gift of exhortation is often called the "gift of encouragement." The Greek word for this gift is *parakaleo*. It means to beseech, exhort, call upon, to encourage and to strengthen. The primary means of exhortation is to remind the hearer of the powerful and amazing work of God in Christ, particularly in regard to the saving work of Jesus in the atonement. We see Paul commanding Titus to use this gift in Titus 1:9 and throughout chapter 2, particularly Titus 2:11–15. He also charges Timothy in 2 Timothy 4:2. The Spirit

of God gives this gift to people in the church to strengthen and encourage those who are wavering in their faith. Those with the gift of exhortation can uplift and motivate others as well as challenge and rebuke them in order to foster spiritual growth and action. The goal of the encourager is to see everyone in the church continually building up the body of Christ and glorifying God. [6]

Now, I'll stray off topic for a moment to conclude this chapter with a valuable lesson. We all come to a season where trials bring us to our knees and attempt to shake our faith. I know from experience it's critical to have at least one good friend to be present through the turbulent storms. We need someone trustworthy and compassionate, someone who'll listen without judgment when we vent our frustrations and confess our sins. Most importantly, we need encouragement. I thank the Lord for my personal mentor, who fits this description.

It was at this point in my life where I was reminded this is what it's all about—to build the kingdom of God by sharing my testimony. How could I remain silent when He rescued my soul? Because of that, I profess God's love and faithfulness, keeping His promises to those who place their trust in Him. Even in the midst of traumatic circumstances, He remains in control and desires the best for His beloved children.

> So, do not be afraid of them, for there is nothing concealed that will not be disclosed, or hidden that will not be made known. What I tell you in the dark, speak in the daylight; what is whispered in your ear, proclaim from the roofs. Do not be afraid of those who kill the body but cannot kill the soul. Rather, be afraid of the One who can destroy both soul and body in hell. Are not two sparrows sold for a penny? Yet not one of them will fall to the ground outside your Father's care. And even the very hairs of your head are all numbered. So, don't be afraid; you are worth more than many sparrows. Whoever acknowledges me before others, I will also acknowledge before my Father in heaven. But whoever disowns me before others, I will disown before my Father in heaven. (Matt. 10:26–33 NIV)

While I knew and understood these truths, there remained times I wanted to turn my back on God and yell out to Him in anger and frustration, pitifully similar to that of a temper tantrum–throwing toddler. For example, I continued to struggle with resentment against Kyle because he hadn't apologized for what he did. It was obvious I hadn't fully forgiven him. In moments where I stray from the narrow path, God lovingly takes me back as I cry out for mercy and forgiveness. His kindness truly leads us to repentance (Rom. 2:4). He reveals the areas in which I err and teaches me how to overcome those obstacles. It's all part of the transformation process which God promises to His children. "He who began a good work in you will carry it on to completion until the day of Christ Jesus" (Phil. 1:6 NIV)

Oftentimes, I don't reflect Jesus Christ as His followers are expected to, which leads to feelings of shame and disappointment. There's one thing I have to remember when facing those guilty feelings—I was a much different person before Jesus came into my life fourteen years ago (in 2005). I'm still in the stage of transformation, which will continue until my final breath. The key to transformation is awareness. Believers become more aware of their sinfulness through the Holy Spirit, which leads them to repentance. When I engage in sinful behavior, I also suffer the consequences. The Lord reveals warning signs and red flags, but ultimately, I'm the one who decides which path to take. I have the free will to decide, even though I occasionally make the wrong decisions.

As children of God, we're subject to His righteous discipline. When I start to feel angry at Him for my afflictions, I redirect my focus on the reasons behind the affliction. "What is the Lord trying to teach me?" God's Word is the answer to that question. To understand discipline, we must look at what the Word says:

> In your struggle against sin, you have not yet resisted to the point of shedding your blood. And

have you completely forgotten this word of encouragement that addresses you as a father addresses his son? It says, "My son, do not make light of the Lord's discipline, and do not lose heart when he rebukes you, because the Lord disciplines the one he loves, and he chastens everyone he accepts as his son." Endure hardship as discipline; God is treating you as his children. For what children are not disciplined by their father? If you are not disciplined—and everyone undergoes discipline—then you are not legitimate, not true sons and daughters at all. Moreover, we have all had human fathers who disciplined us and we respected them for it. How much more should we submit to the Father of spirits and live! They disciplined us for a little while as they thought best; but God disciplines us for our good, in order that we may share in his holiness. No discipline seems pleasant at the time, but painful. Later on, however, it produces a harvest of righteousness and peace for those who have been trained by it. (Heb. 12:4–11 NIV)

All Scripture is God breathed and is useful for teaching, rebuking, correcting and training in righteousness, so that the servant of God may be thoroughly equipped for every good work. (2 Tim. 3:16–17 NIV)

LIFE LESSON

Those who disregard discipline despise themselves, but the one who heeds correction gains understanding. (Pro. 15:32 NIV)

13

THROWN INTO THE FIRE TO BE REFINED

Toward the end of September 2017, I received an unexpected phone call. A relative of mine, Curtis, said he needed a place to stay until he saved enough money to move into an apartment. His request caught me off guard, and I knew it wouldn't be a good idea to let him stay with us. Our worldviews and lifestyles differed, and I worried about the potential effect it might have on Damon. However, since Curtis was a relative, I allowed him to move in. We came to the agreement he'd pay a small portion of his paychecks throughout his stay. This was to help him save as much as possible for his own place. I made my expectations clear, and he expressed understanding. It wouldn't be long before I realized I had made a mistake.

After leaving the field of social work in October 2017 to begin employment at the plant, I felt relief. I had an opportunity to get to know new people in what I thought was a less stressful environment. The atmosphere was something I needed to adjust to because I was accustomed to an atmosphere of prayer, support, love, and sharing Christ openly. This plant was your typical factory where cursing, dirty humor, and gossip were common.

I prepared myself for this in advance, being determined not to get lured back into the darkness. I lived in it before and didn't want to go back! I believed I was strong enough to stand firm and resist the devil's attacks. I was set in treating others with kindness and respect, something uncommon in your typical factory. I prayed fervently as I got ready for work each morning to help prepare for whatever would come my way. I asked for a chance to talk about the Lord with whoever He saw fit, and it was granted to me. I was able to share my testimony with two coworkers in the same day and praised God for the opportunity. I openly shared my unwavering faith with others without fear of judgment. I didn't care if it cost me. I believe Satan was threatened by this and started to work against me.

On October 23, 2017 I had a frightening nightmare. I dreamed I walked into a dark, dungeon type room, which I believe was intended to be Damon's bedroom. I saw a grey and black figure sitting on what appeared to be a throne. It could've been Satan as he represented pure evil. The atmosphere of wickedness overwhelmed me as I walked in. There was also a heaviness which seemed to hold me down. In this dream, I attempted to pray in Jesus's name, but I was unable to speak. After much persistence, I was eventually able to do so. I woke up and prayed for Jesus to cast out any evil spirits around us. It's imperative to speak out in prayer because that's where the power lies. I have noticed if I keep silent and don't speak out, I feel powerless against the enemy's attacks.

On November 15, I had another nightmare. This one involved another evil spirit, similar to the last one. It took place in an unfamiliar dark, dusty, and abandoned house. I looked through the rooms and came to a place where I felt a strong presence of evil. I saw a shadowy figure move, and as I said the name of Jesus repeatedly, it growled at me. The growl was deep and scary, the kind you'd hear in a horror movie.

Deep down, I wondered if the dreams represented Curtis staying in Damon's room and potentially bringing demonic spirits into our house. It didn't take long for me to realize I made a poor decision allowing him to stay with us. A negative energy soon replaced the positive one that once filled our home. I no longer felt the presence of the Lord, which provided an ambience of peace, joy, and contentment.

Instead, the ambience was replaced with tension, negativity, and drama.

I knew I was going to have to make a tough decision. I wanted him out for a few reasons. First, I needed my home to be a peaceful refuge, not a place of tension. Second, Curtis attempted to pit our family members against each other, causing division. Third, and most importantly, he wasn't saving any money. It appeared he was using me as he had done with other relatives. I had no other choice but to move his things out after the new year. Out of respect, I waited until after Christmas. Once Curtis was out, I prayed fervently throughout my house to restore the once peaceful atmosphere. Finally, my home felt back to normal.

It's interesting how I was aware of the change in environment, confirming the reality of spiritual warfare. As I grew stronger in relationship with my Abba Father, it seemed I became more aware of my surroundings in a spiritual sense. Over the last year, I did so well in my walk with the Lord that none of Satan's attacks were effective.

Unfortunately, the devil wasn't finished messing with me. He began attacking through my job, which spilled over into other areas of my life. I was brought to exhaustion working a great deal of mandatory overtime. For weeks I'd have only Sunday off, but one day off was never for rest. I kept busy catching up with household responsibilities and taking care of Damon, which resulted in placing God on the backburner. As you might expect, my physical health took a turn for the worst. In late January 2018, I was moved to a new position in another department, performing much heftier tasks throughout the entire day. This proved physically challenging for someone my size, especially with all of the required overtime.

The heavy assembly work I was expected to perform was not appropriate for someone my size and proved to be harmful. It led me to experience pain and numbness on an increasing level, resulting from substantial overuse. I woke up in the middle of the night to a numbing, fiery sensation in my hands, lasting around five minutes. I had never experienced pain like this before, so I was quite concerned. I also developed common cold symptoms. I rarely came down with a cold, but if I did, it would be this time of year. Thankfully, I already scheduled an appointment to establish care with a new primary doctor.

It was pretty evident God was no longer on the throne of my heart and the center of my life. I didn't recognize the importance of this issue until it was too late. At the time, I thought I had valid excuses to procrastinate, but they were quite pitiful. I was "too busy" to meditate on His Word, "too distracted" to engage in daily prayer, and "too exhausted" to listen to His voice and instruction for my wellbeing. This gradual decline inevitably led to natural consequences.

Kind of sounds familiar doesn't it? I previously pointed my finger toward someone else for using those same excuses.

Prior to these attacks on my health, I signed up for a five week long Bible study at our new church. I wanted to become more involved and get to know others in the church. It was conveniently scheduled after Sunday service, one of the only days I was guaranteed off work. Of course, the enemy wanted to throw a wrench under the bus because he knows it doesn't take much to discourage me. The first week, I was unable to find the classroom and ended up not going. The second week I made it to class and received homework. As I attempted to work on the questions, I was unable to focus. The third week is when I experienced my sickness and didn't want to risk getting others sick, so I told the instructor I wasn't going to make it.

Feeling discouraged and ashamed of myself, I cancelled the study. I already missed two of the five classes and figured there was no point completing the course. Deep down, I desired to get back on track, however, it seemed Satan was winning in everything. As months passed, I became progressively more discouraged. My body became physically weak, pain continued, and new symptoms developed. My primary and occupational doctors refused to properly address the issue, so I continued to work in pain.

My strong willed pride took a fall. I was once a strong, independent, single mother who could do anything. Now, I was dependent on other people to help take care of me, including Damon! I'm glad I had a support system in place to help me get through this.

It got to the point where it looked as if the world was against me. My employer expressed no sympathy, refused to answer valid questions or assist me in navigating resources to address my injury. The medical professionals I turned to for healing blew off my concerns. Their only solution was to take anti inflammatory medications, which proved ineffective. All I wanted was to be treated like a human being and get healed!

I felt I was hitting a dead end and wanted to give up. In May 2018, I fought the temptation to walk out the door and quit. There were multiple occasions where this internal war took place, but I always gathered enough strength to keep trudging through. Something deep down told me to hold on, which I knew was the Holy Spirit.

I had an upcoming appointment with a new doctor located at a different medical facility. I decided to go with another provider since the one I initially went to refused to properly handle the issue. I was relieved to find a doctor who cared about my situation and desired to help me heal. Eventually, through his care plan, my constant pain reduced drastically.

LIFE LESSON

While I still experienced occasional symptoms, I was able to get back to the normal life I once had. Hope was restored.

14

THE LORD NEVER CEASES TO SPEAK

As I continued to work for my toxic employer, I valued the importance of maintaining regular church attendance. Being exposed to negativity on a daily basis led me to crave a positive atmosphere. It was a breath of fresh air—the one thing I looked forward to. I occasionally took notes during church service on anything I felt the Lord revealed to me. They were often revelations related to the sermon, or a random thought that popped in my head. One of the things I wrote down was: The Lord made His presence known to me some mornings ago, and though He knew I'd sin against Him last night (after making His presence known), He loves me enough to still reveal Himself to me! How great is the love the Father has lavished unto us!

No matter how many times I fail, even in the same sin, God still cares. He expresses His love and patience with me. As I learned to better understand grace, the chains of guilt no longer held me down as it did in the past. I realized God's grace applies to me, too. I know I'm unworthy, but He doesn't treat me as such. When I think about God's grace, I can't help but compare it to His vast oceans. Throughout my life, I often dreamed about tidal waves and rising waters. I have a major fear of drowning, but His grace overcomes fear. It's greater than the depths of the seas and covers the overwhelming floods of our sinfulness. Jesus has the power to either calm the storms in our life, or to comfort us during the storms as they rage all around us.

> Then he got into the boat and his disciples followed him. Suddenly a furious storm came up on the lake, so that the waves swept over the boat. But Jesus was sleeping. The disciples went and woke him, saying, "Lord, save us! We're going to drown!" He replied, "You of little faith, why are you so afraid?" Then he got up and rebuked the winds and the waves, and it was completely calm. The men were amazed and asked, "What kind of man is this? Even the winds and the waves obey him!" (Mat. 8:23–27 NIV)

God continued to use this church as a means to reveal Himself to me. I initially wondered why the Lord led us to switch, and it now became clear. During reflection time one Sunday, I closed my eyes and immediately saw an image. It was a black shadow in the form of a man on one knee, reaching His hand out to me. I knew exactly who it was and felt abundant peace. John 10:14 (NIV) says, "I am the good shepherd; I know my sheep and my sheep know me."

While navigating the stormy season of uncertainty within my job, I received another reassurance from the Lord. If we pay close attention to the small details, we'll begin to recognize key words relayed through repetition. My key word on May 6, 2018 was fear. It originated on social media, when a friend shared a passage with me: "So do not fear, for I am with you; do not be dismayed, for I am your God. I will strengthen you and help you; I will uphold you with my righteous right hand" (Isaiah 41:10 NIV).

This same passage came up in the pastor's sermon. He provided scripture related to overcoming fear, primarily related to sharing Jesus with others (Acts 18:9–10; Joshua 1:5–6, 9; Jeremiah 1:6–8). Jesus's presence is what helps us overcome our fears. We must trust in the will of God.

For me, a repetitious theme given at least three times is confirmation. After service, I turned the radio on in my car and a song came on about fear. I couldn't help but find humor in this. At the same time, I didn't realize how much fear was plaguing me. Where did my faith go? Where was my trust in the Almighty God who rescued me time and time again?

Not only had I feared my circumstances but I feared God wouldn't work in the midst of them. The presence of evil filled my workplace. It felt the years of progress I made went out the window. The plant's negativity and drama latched onto me, and I couldn't release its grip. I was losing a battle that was never mine to fight. Due to lack of prayer and communion with God, I reverted back to many of my old ways and was ashamed. It felt like I was in too deep and couldn't get out. I reflected back on those dreams I had in the autumn season. Initially, I thought the dreams represented Curtis's presence in our home, but now I wondered if it was a warning about my new occupation.

God spoke yet again. After service on August 12, 2018, I pulled out my sermon notes to see if there was anything I could use in my book. The sermon focused on God's Word in scripture. As I reviewed my book, I came across a sentence that struck me: "The last two years were a living hell, and though I was told it was going to be so great after my suffering was done, my belief in that disappeared." I began to meditate on where my life was at its lowest point and where it is now. The life I now live is much greater than the temporary suffering I endured those two years. My employer was nothing compared to homelessness and abandonment!

My perspective on life changed the more I understood how much God loves and cares for me. My needs have always been provided for. My current blessings were much greater than the things that were initially taken from me (similar to the book of Job). God promised the suffering would last for a little while. At the time, I couldn't see it because all I saw was the suffering and pain. The discouragement I felt about my current job and physical health couldn't compare to my past experiences. I'd been through worse, and God always saw me through it. Why didn't I consider this?

Back to the sermon about God's Word: His Word stands, transforms, and refines us. He spoke the universe into existence for crying out loud! God's Word is powerful and the source of life itself. I trust in God's Word because of the mounting evidence I personally witnessed from the moment I got saved from death.

> Having purified your souls by your obedience to the truth for a sincere brotherly love, love one another earnestly from a pure heart, since you have been born again, not of perishable seed but of imperishable, through the living and abiding word of God; for 'All flesh is like grass and all its glory like the flower of grass. The grass withers, and the flower falls, but the word of the Lord remains forever.' And this word is the good news that was preached to you. (1 Pet. 1:22–25 NIV)

Once I snapped back into reality, remembering the truth of God's promises through His Word, I felt a bit of contentment. I understood there was a reason God led me to this employer, and while I couldn't fully see it just yet, I knew I'd gain understanding in retrospect. I asked God to let me know when He wanted me to move on and prayed to have enough strength to not walk out when I've had enough. I wanted to leave the company when it was the Lord's time, not mine, so I continued to wait patiently. In November 2018, I received what I believed to be a hint from the Lord. Not to say He always speaks through fortune cookies, but the coincidence and how it applied to my situation had me cracking up. I thought "only the Lord could've sent this!"

The fortune cookie read: "You are soon going to change your present line of work." This was the third fortune cookie to make me laugh, seeing God's potential hand in it. The first two had the exact same message, and I received them consecutively, one in late April 2018 and the other in early June 2018. Those messages read: "You need not worry about your future." As silly as it may sound, I felt reassured that God had it all under control. I want to make it clear, I don't put my trust in other avenues outside of God's Word, such as horoscopes and fortune telling. But for some reason, I knew it was a hint from my heavenly Father.

It wouldn't be until December 2018 when those tiny messages began to stir in my heart. I paid attention to my life outside of my job. It wasn't much of a life, seeing how a majority of my time was spent at work. I was always too exhausted to do things I enjoyed or pay attention to Damon. I figured since he was going on thirteen, he's independent enough to handle things like schoolwork on his own.

Unfortunately, the reality was he needed his mother now more than ever, heading into adolescence. There were several indications that this matter needed to be addressed. He'd been engaging in attention seeking behaviors for quite some time, and I often told him to "stop trying to get attention!" It reflected in his grades as he also sought attention from those at school, typically with silly behavior. Let's face it; he was the class clown.

In this moment though, I knew there was an underlying issue I needed to concentrate on. When I asked Damon why he was attention seeking, if it was because I wasn't giving him enough attention, he confirmed—yes. I felt so guilty. Somehow, I recalled my journal entry from 9/14/16 where the Lord told me to "focus on Damon—it's especially critical now." Two years had passed since that entry and I failed to consistently place it as a priority. Being a single mother is tough, but it's no excuse to overlook what's most important. I wondered, *How in the world could I dedicate the time necessary to help Damon succeed*? Something had to change.

As I spent time considering what was more important in life, I noticed my book had been neglected throughout the time I worked for this employer. Knowing how important it was to get this story out, I realized my job prevented me from accomplishing God's will. And speaking of God, I continued to place Him on the backburner! He's supposed to be the center of my focus—always. After getting injured and trying various medications, the side effect of constant drowsiness caused me to feel unmotivated, which led to discouragement. As a result, I put my writing off, even though the Lord gently urged me to continue. Thankfully, during the summer I decided to cut the medication, and my motivation eventually returned.

It became evident the longer I stayed, the unhappier I felt. Things weren't getting better; they were getting worse. I mean this in a spiritual sense, but it also affected me physically, mentally, and emotionally. Work seemed to drain the life right out of me. I had to rearrange my priorities, and the time was now. Upon recognition of these three critical factors—time with God, Damon, and the completion of my book—I decided to put in my notice. One thing I knew for certain was I didn't want to bring this negativity into the new year. I wanted to start fresh in 2019, focusing on what would give God the glory.

The timing was perfect. I turned in my resignation on December 3, which gave the company a three week notice.

Even though I didn't have a job lined up, I knew I didn't have to worry about my future. I'd been through this enough to know Jehovah Jireh ("The Lord who provides") always has my back. I planned on withdrawing my 401k, and tax return season was coming upon us. This gave me an opportunity to dedicate as much time as possible to focus on restoring my health, paying more attention to Damon, prayer, and my writing. In the meantime, I kept an eye out for job postings in a different setting. I didn't want to go back to having a caseload, so I avoided social work listings, and I no longer wanted to work in manufacturing. I prayed the Lord would help me through this season.

Following my last day, I noticed an immediate sense of relief, and an enormous burden was lifted. It took around three whole weeks for me to fully recover from the negativity of my former employer. I knew I made the right decision because I needed to take care of these crucial tasks. It surprised me how quickly my book was coming together. I knew it was time to put an end to the story because God, in His faithfulness, revealed that it was now time. You know something is meant to be when a random, out of the blue, event takes place. I received a call from someone whose wife recently published a book. When we connected, she offered tips and advice, which helped significantly. I didn't know anything about publishing a book, but God provided the resources.

It was nice being able to spend more time with Damon. I was able to stay on him about organizing his schoolwork. I encouraged him to read more books and study better for tests. We also got back into our routine of playing board games, which is our favorite thing to do in the dreary winter season. I even dragged him to my walking paths, so we could both get our exercise in. Damon expressed appreciation for my efforts, and I apologized for not being able to do so before.

I developed a daily routine during the week, making sure to meet my goals. It helped keep me accountable and continue to focus on what needed to be done. In the midst of all this, I didn't receive one call from any employer I submitted my resume to. It didn't surprise me because I knew the Lord had me where He wanted me. While I don't know what the future holds, I rest assured in my Father's loving arms. He's protected me from dangers, seen and unseen, for a purpose. Being only thirty six years old, my story will carry on. I'll continue to learn lessons through time and experience. Life isn't easy, but it's much better when you allow Jesus to be a part of it. "I've told you these things, so that in me you may have peace. In this world you will have trouble. But take heart! I have overcome the world" (John 16:33 NIV).

15
LIFE LESSONS

My final chapter begins by focusing on two words—*humility* and *wisdom*. As you can see, I've discovered many important lessons through various trials and blessings. It required humility to seek God and submit to His will. Humility didn't come easily because it involved surrender, letting go of my pride. It also required wisdom, which often comes with age and experience. If you've made mistakes in your life, chances are you learn from them in the hope you won't make the same mistake twice. If you're like me, you might make the same mistake several times! Thankfully, as I grew older and experienced recurrent failure and rejection, I learned how to be well prepared for life's curveballs.

The Bible is full of verses related to humility and wisdom. Here are just a few:

> When pride comes, then comes disgrace, but with humility comes wisdom. (Prov. 11:2 NIV)

> Wisdom's instruction is to fear the Lord, and humility comes before honor. (Prov. 15:33 NIV)

> Is not wisdom found among the aged? Does not long life bring understanding? (Job 12:12 NIV)

> Who is wise and understanding among you? Let them show it by their good life, by deeds done in the humility that comes from wisdom. (Jas 3:13 NIV)

I appreciate the valuable things I learned as a young adult. I often wonder where I'd be in life if I had continued to walk on the path of destruction (before getting saved). I could've made some terrible decisions, but it doesn't help to think about the "what ifs." What matters is what I am doing with those lessons. As you can see, I turned them into a book. I'll conclude my story, summing up just a few of the most important things I've discovered over the years. They're in no particular order. Bear in mind, these are personal reflections.

1. Life consists of meaning and purpose. The Lord took it upon Himself to save me from the pit of despair. He saw me in my desperate and lonely place. I begged for death to end the misery, yet He

answered my plea: "I wish I had a reason to live." If my life had no meaning or purpose, He wouldn't have spared me and given me a story to tell. We're all here for a purpose; we just need to pay attention to where the Lord is leading us.

2. When things don't seem to go my way, or how I'd expect them to go, I no longer get upset. I consider if there's potential danger lurking ahead. Maybe the Lord is providing me with a U turn for a reason. Sometimes, what we want isn't what's always best for us, but our heavenly Father always knows what's best, and He wants to see us succeed. Patient endurance is a valuable trait. The Lord shows *great* patience for His children, so we should show Him the same respect.

3. Many people come and go in one's life for a purpose. Sometimes they'll leave you with positive experiences, and sometimes they'll leave you with negative experiences. I learned who my true friends were when going through times of suffering. Real friends won't abandon you at your worst. Anyone who remains faithful in encouragement, seeing your flaws and loving you anyway, are those worth keeping around. Let go of anyone who doesn't lift you up in love. We're all imperfect because we

struggle with sin, so we have to try not to hold grudges against those who have done us wrong.

4. Forgiveness is critical for my wellbeing, in order to successfully move on to healing. We'll inevitably be hurt by people, whether friends, family, spouses, colleagues, neighbors, strangers, and so forth. It's important to try to forgive those who've caused us the most harm. They may be the ones who'll never ask for our forgiveness, but in order for our burden of pain to be lifted, we have to let go of the circumstances by forgiving them. It doesn't mean we have to allow them back into our lives, especially if it's not safe to do so. It also doesn't mean we should forget what they've done. Remembrance helps me learn how to not make the same mistake twice. I don't want history repeating itself. I also don't want to be stuck with feelings of bitterness and resentment. I'll provide verses on forgiveness for your reference if you want to spend time looking more into them: Gen. 50:15–21, Matt. 6:14–15, Matt. 18:21–35, Mark 11:25, Luke 6:37–42, Luke 17:3–4, 2 Cor. 2:5–11, and Col. 3:13.

5. When I look at Damon and hear him talk about Jesus, I couldn't be prouder. He truly is God's own child, and I can only imagine what the future holds for him. When Damon was young, I asked

the Lord to be his Father because I didn't know anything about being a parent. I didn't know how to be both a mother and a father to him, so I entrusted Damon's life to the Lord's hands. To this day, it remains one of the smartest decisions I've ever made.

6. As time goes on, I keep receiving a better understanding of who God is, and our relationship is continuing to grow stronger as I increasingly desire to live in obedience to His will. My experiences have brought me closer to the Lord and opened my eyes to a lot of amazing things. It's important to find a Bible teaching church in order to grow in knowledge of our Creator. Unfortunately, not all churches teach the Bible or preach the truth of God's Word. The only way you'll be able to discern this for yourself is by reading God's Word yourself. The Bible warns Christians not to fall for deceptive teachings (Mat. 7:15–20; Rom. 16:17–19; 1 Tim. 6:3–5; 2 Tim. 4:3–4; Col. 2:8). If you attend a church where you're not convicted of sin, then it's time to move on. I've had to pass on a few when I needed to find a new church after relocating because of those reasons.

7. Speaking out the praises of God brings joy to the soul. In the time I felt I was held down by the

negative forces in my former work environment, praise seemed to have escaped my lips. Even after I left, I noticed I had to reintroduce praise into my routine. During times I was closest to the Lord, praise came naturally and brought much peace and contentment. When I strayed off course, praise was no longer natural, and I had to force it back. Consequently, the peace, joy, and contentment left when the praises stopped. I also realized that the type of entertainment you allow in your life affects your mood. For years, I listened to genres of music with evil lyrics and messages. Once I incorporated Christian praise and worship music into my life, I noticed a difference in my mood. The same goes for other avenues of entertainment, such as movies, television shows, and so on. I encourage you to surround yourself with positive messages through the entertainment industry. It makes a huge difference.

8. As I continued to experience pain and rejection through various relationships, hoping to find a husband, I eventually realized I had made an idol of marriage. I wanted it more than anything, even though I knew the Lord was sufficient enough for me. I have to wait for His timing, with the man He has in store for me. I always pray for His will to be done, and it's especially important in this area. I shouldn't worry about finding a husband anyway

> because His Word says in Isaiah 54:5 (NIV): "For your Maker is your husband, the Lord Almighty is His name, the Holy One of Israel is your Redeemer, He is called the God of all the earth."

I heard a pastor say during a sermon, when you go from darkness to light, it's for a purpose. You were saved for a reason, and that reason is to proclaim the Gospel. We cannot be silent when we understand what God has rescued us from. This is the exact reason I wrote my testimony.

The person I was before God stepped in is not the person I would've wanted to be for the rest of my life. I previously lived a life without hope or direction. I lived life for my own glory, but we weren't created to do that. We were created to worship God, for His glory, because He *alone* is holy and worthy of our praise.

If I hadn't made the decision to turn to God in the midst of my attempted suicide, who knows where I would've ended up? He allowed me to hit rock bottom because that's what it took to wake me up and shake me from the chains, which held me down for so long. I had nowhere else to turn *but* God, as He waited patiently to take me into His loving arms, adopting me as His own to transform me more and more into His image.

Readers, may you find and treasure the Lord's peace, love, and blessings into your hearts. Always remember that He loves you *dearly* and wants to spend eternity with you. It's ultimately your choice to accept the Lord's invitation to spend eternity with Him.

> If you declare with your mouth, "Jesus is Lord," and believe in your heart that God raised him from the dead, you will be saved. For it is with your heart that you believe and are justified, and it is with your mouth that you profess your faith and are saved. As Scripture says, "Anyone who believes in him will never be put to shame." For there is no difference between Jew and Gentile, the same Lord is Lord of all and richly blesses all who call on him, for, "Everyone who calls on the name of the Lord will be saved." (Rom. 10:9–13 NIV)

RECOMMENDED READINGS

(Website articles can change at any time.)

- o "Top 10 Emotions People Commonly Feel During (and after) a Narcissistically Abusive Relationship," Dana Morningstar, June 3, 2016, Copyright © 2019 | MH Magazine WordPress. https://www.thriveafterabuse.com/top-10-emotions-people-commonly-feel-during-and-after-a-narcissistically-abusive-relationship/?fbclid=IwAR0jp_nUr0Q3F-WCI1y3s_N2Y-19IRDOW0dH6S5hWq-0D_wY5DC1GdLp85Ss

- o "Four Mistakes We Often Make When Life Doesn't Make Sense," Sarah Walton, May 11, 2015. Unlocking the Bible, 2018. http://unlockingthebible.org/2015/05/when-life-doesnt-make-sense

- "10 Biblical Keys to Staying Positive in the Midst of Trials," Joshua Infantado, September 5, 2017. Becoming Christians. https://becomingchristians.com/2017/09/05/10-biblical-keys-to-staying-positive-in-the-midst-of-trials/

- Goodman, Karon P. *You're Late Again, Lord! The Impatient Woman's Guide to God's Timing*. Uhrichsville: Barbour Books, 2002.

NOTES

1: M. G. Easton MA, DD, *Illustrated Bible Dictionary*, Third Edition, published by Thomas Nelson, 1897. Public Domain. https://www.biblestudytools.com/dictionary/saint/

2: Thomas Moore. AZQuotes.com, Wind and Fly LTD, 2019. https://www.azquotes.com/quote/353456, accessed February 25, 2019.

3: Karon P. Goodman. *You're Late Again, Lord! The Impatient Woman's Guide to God's Timing.* (Uhrichsville: Barbour Books, 2002).

4: NIV Thinline Bible. *Busy Mom's Edition.* (Grand Rapids: Zondervan Publishing House, 2009), "Your Relationships," 438–9.

5: NIV Thinline Bible. *Busy Mom's Edition,* 1152, 1157.

6: Spiritual Gifts Test, 2019. *https://spiritualgiftstest.com/spiritual-gifts*

CPSIA information can be obtained
at www.ICGtesting.com
Printed in the USA
LVHW080934301021
701969LV00022B/375